How to Be Radical in Philosophy

Also Available from Bloomsbury

The Meaning of Life and Death, Michael Hauskeller
How to Be a Philosopher, Gary Cox
Dying for Ideas, Costica Bradatan

How to Be Radical in Philosophy

Maximilian de Gaynesford

BLOOMSBURY ACADEMIC
LONDON • NEW YORK • OXFORD • NEW DELHI • SYDNEY

BLOOMSBURY ACADEMIC
Bloomsbury Publishing Plc
50 Bedford Square, London, WC1B 3DP, UK
1385 Broadway, New York, NY 10018, USA
29 Earlsfort Terrace, Dublin 2, Ireland

BLOOMSBURY, BLOOMSBURY ACADEMIC and the Diana logo are trademarks
of Bloomsbury Publishing Plc

First published in Great Britain 2023

Cover design by Tjaša Krivec

A catalogue record for this book is available from the British Library.

A catalog record for this book is available from the Library of Congress.

ISBN: HB: 978-1-3503-3701-5
PB: 978-1-3503-3700-8
ePDF: 978-1-3503-3702-2
eBook: 978-1-3503-3703-9

Typeset by Deanta Global Publishing Services, Chennai, India
Printed and bound in Great Britain

To find out more about our authors and books visit www.bloomsbury.com and
sign up for our newsletters.

Contents

Introduction

Philosophy is radical when it is audacious and engaged with fundamental issues that matter to us all about how the world is and how we should live in it. This book will achieve its aim if it supports you in doing radical philosophy, should you be so motivated.

There is an urgent call for it.

At the end of February 2022, as I write, governments are failing to agree on the most basic measures necessary to prevent imminent environmental catastrophe, the world is entering nervously into a third year of life under profound civil restrictions to cope with the Covid pandemic, the foremost military and economic power in the world is still grappling to understand how its seat of government in the US Capitol could have been stormed by supporters of the then president at his own behest and today – 24 February 2022 – Russian Federation forces under the orders of President Vladimir Putin have invaded Ukraine on multiple fronts, striking civilian sites as well as military targets, capturing the dark sarcophagus of Chernobyl and approaching the northern outskirts of the capital Kyiv, prompting the Secretary General of NATO Jens Stoltenberg to prophesy that these acts will have 'shattered the peace of Europe'.

If we truly want to face up to our present condition – not only the wrenching transformations in the recent past that have brought us to it, but the magnitude of the changes that it will require of us in the immediate and long-term future – we need to ask some fundamental questions about how the world is and how we should live in it. These are the questions we shall be asking:

What can we know, and how? (Chapter 1)
What kind of thing are we? (Chapter 2)
How are we related to the material world? (Chapter 3)

If we can face up to these questions, they lead to others that come even closer to home:

> *What do we need to live a genuinely human existence? (Chapter 4)*
> *Should we replace our present political and economic system? (Chapter 5)*
> *How and why do we mislead ourselves about what is in our best interests?*
> *(Chapter 6)*

And once we have looked these issues in the face, we are ready for questions that are most truly intimate while still being philosophical:

> *What grounds our everyday ways of living in the world? (Chapter 7)*
> *Is it possible for us to live in an authentic way? (Chapter 8)*
> *How should we face our own death? (Chapter 9)*

Engaging with these fundamental questions makes this a book of philosophy. But there is more to it than that. Facing up to our critical present calls for us to be *audacious* in engaging with these fundamental questions that matter to us all, renouncing what is conventional, orthodox, predictable or established and offering alternatives instead that are new, original, creative and surprising. That is what makes it a book of *radical* philosophy.

There are several different ways to be audacious about fundamental issues that matter. I do not think we yet know which is the best for facing up to our critical present. So that is what gives the book its purpose: to compare different tested ways of being radical in philosophy so as to determine which, if any, to follow.

The five different tested ways we shall be exploring correspond with five different strategies that modern philosophy uses to refashion itself and thus stay radically engaged with what matters. It is the details of the differences that will concern us, but for now some more superficial labelling must suffice. The five strategies take their stand respectively on *Reason, Experience, Action, Analysis* and *Self-Criticism.*

Each of these ways can be associated with various philosophers, but we shall focus on one each for simplicity and focus.

René Descartes (*Chapters 1–2*) will represent those who take their stand on Reason, though we might equally have chosen others like Spinoza or Leibniz.

John Locke (*Chapter 3*) will be the focus when we consider taking a stand on Experience, though Berkeley or Hume would also have been good partners.

For Action, Aristotle or Hobbes recommend themselves, but we will focus on Karl Marx (*Chapter 4–5*).

For Analysis, Russell or G. E. Moore would have been good candidates as ancestors of present-day analytic philosophy, but we shall do the more fittingly radical thing and focus instead on an equally apt philosopher from a very different tradition: Theodor Adorno (*Chapter 6*).

Finally, for Self-Criticism, many radical philosophers from Plato through Kant to Wittgenstein might have served, but again with a radical approach in mind, we shall face up to the most difficult and unnerving case of those who take their stand here: Martin Heidegger (*Chapters 7–9*).

What unites these five ways of being radical in philosophy is that each is extraordinarily new, original, creative and surprising – audacious – in seeking out the roots of things and in engaging thoroughly in issues that matter to everyone. But another more disturbing connection stands out as the book progresses. Each starts by identifying something disastrously wrong with previous philosophizing and heads out in a daringly opposed direction, but each then finds itself bogged down in the very impasse it tried to escape.

Hence there is a paradox at the very heart of the book. We need philosophy to be radical if it is to stay relevant and connected, but this urge to be radical threatens to undermine philosophy itself.

We can call this 'the Trojan Horse syndrome' because it recalls the way Troy fell: the inhabitants became unwitting authors of their own downfall by drawing the enemy into the heart of their city, concealed within a wooden horse.

This is a deeply unsettling main theme with many troubling implications. But that is what we should expect of a book that aims to practise radical philosophy on radical philosophy.

The book is radical in other ways also. In particular, it seeks to enable very different philosophical traditions to talk fruitfully to each other. This means gathering together very different philosophers who are usually kept strictly separate from each other. It means trying to overcome the differences which keep professional gulfs in place. This includes differences in method and style which keep groups like 'Analytic' and 'Continental' philosophers apart. It also includes differences in content and approach which keep categories like 'Theoretical' and 'Practical' philosophy apart. The book works hard to help overcome these divisions because we need to unify where we can if we are to engage with the concrete, fundamental problems of living, working, thinking and dying.

The method of the book is radical also: to enable readers to philosophize for themselves rather than simply handing them the results. The point of radical philosophy is like the taste of food; you just don't get it unless you do the chewing yourself.

So the book is as an exercise of philosophy, not a history of it. It is not a history of ideas or a biography of philosophers, still less a polemic in favour of some and against others. It is not a standard introduction or conventional contribution to scholarship. It is a book *of* radical philosophy, not *about* radical philosophy. It resists the temptation to anticipate and forestall each of the reader's thoughts and objections. It tries instead to support their thinking with prompts and challenges, sometimes by adopting quite radical interpretations. It tries to stimulate readers to think for themselves and gives them the resources to start doing so. It employs the usual devices – textual focus, supportive commentary, exploratory thought – but in ways that remain open-ended. Wherever the book comes to a point where readers divide – some asking, *How does this way of seeing what NN means help with our fundamental questions?* and others asking, *Did NN really mean this?* – it will give preference to the first group.

The underlying aim of the book is simple and practical: to help enable us to face up to the crises of our present by encouraging us to address the fundamental issues that previous radical philosophers have faced, to work alongside them, learning from them where possible and jettisoning them where necessary, with the prospect of puzzling through to some answers of our own.

My heartfelt thanks to colleagues and students, past and present, for their curiosity, enthusiasm and generosity over the thirty years I have been teaching philosophy. I have gained much from discussing various different aspects of radical philosophy with Jon Beale, Chris Borg, Gary Browning, John Cottingham, Peter Dennis, Laura Ekstrom, Judith Katz, Gerald Lang, Chris Miller, Michael Rosen, Scott Sturgeon and Daniel Talbot. Constantine Sandis deserves my special thanks for his warm support with this book as with much else. I am also most grateful to five anonymous reviewers and to Liza Thompson for their painstaking scrutiny and wise advice, and to Lucy Russell and all those involved in producing the book for their care. The book is dedicated to my daughter Elisabeth, thirteen in this present year of crisis and getting to grips with a bewilderingly shape-shifting world. I hope some of the ideas may prove in some way helpful as you fare forward.

Above all, do not listen to those who say that doing philosophy is unrealistic or impractical or a luxury in these anxious times. It is a natural and necessary thing to do! The first time I did what I now recognize as philosophy, I was still a child, locked down in the house with my parents and brother while a civil war raged outside, shutters tightly closed and the lights off so as not to give our presence away, the intermittent sounds of gunfire day and night, dependent on a hushed radio for news, emerging five days later past what I already knew were not bundles of old clothes. I vividly remember feeling a persistent tug to think beyond what was immediately happening while space shrank to a windowless corridor in the heart of the house and time expanded to an endless suspended moment. What can we really know when given such meagre and false information? What kind of thing are we, fragile bodies with such powerful minds, such vivid consciousness? How are we – how should we be – related to others and to the world around us? What do we value, and what do we most need for our continued existence? How should we face our life? How should we face our death? Philosophizing was and remains the natural and essential thing to do.

To the radical philosophizing then.

Radical I

Reason

1

How we might enter philosophy

René Descartes (1596–1650) wrote his *Meditations on First Philosophy* (1641) in Latin in 'a corner of North Holland'. The book is short, but the task it sets itself is momentous: to consider all the fundamental things to be discovered by philosophizing.

The *Meditations* is a model of radical philosophy, audacious and engaged with fundamental issues that matter to us all about how the world is and how we should live in it. This sets it apart from many other works of philosophy. Philosophy can be perfectly fundamental without being audacious, for example. It can get to the roots of things (*radix* = root) and yet pursue a conventional, orthodox, predictable or established course. This is not radical philosophy, which must also offer new, original, creative and surprising alternatives. Even this is not enough. Philosophy can be perfectly audacious and engaged with fundamental issues without being radical philosophy. For example, the fundamental issues it is audacious about can be of purely technical or specialized significance or matter only to particular people, an extremist group for example. If philosophy is to be radical, in our sense, it must also be engaged with issues that matter to us all about how the world is and how we should live in it. In short, it is only when all these essential elements combine – audacious, engaged, with fundamental issues that matter to us all about how the world is and how we should live in it – that we have radical philosophy.

Descartes' radical philosophizing begins with autobiography, which is most unconventional in a work of philosophy:

Some years ago I was struck by the large number of falsehoods that I had accepted as true in my childhood, and by the highly doubtful nature of the whole edifice that I had subsequently based on them. (12; all page references in this chapter are to René Descartes' *Meditations on First Philosophy*; see the Bibliography for full details)

We might wonder why he gives us these personal details in a book about the 'first things' in philosophy. But there is an underlying purpose, and it begins to become apparent soon enough:

I realized that it was necessary, once in the course of my life, to demolish everything completely and start again right from the foundations if I wanted to establish anything at all in the sciences that was stable and likely to last. (12)

What Descartes is telling us is that this is going to be a personal quest but one with general scope: to find the foundations for scientific inquiry. And it may have a wider purpose also: to make it possible for others also to pursue such inquiry. Certainly, the reader of his book will be engaging in the same inquiry that Descartes himself once underwent and which he is about to re-enact:

So today I have expressly rid my mind of all worries and arranged for myself a clear stretch of free time. I am here quite alone, and at last will devote myself sincerely and without reservation to the general demolition of my opinions. (12)

The idea that this inquiry should be undertaken 'once in the course of my life' reflects the gravity of the enterprise. Descartes will treat the inquiry as a compelling but strenuous enterprise, not to be undertaken lightly. Again, the proposal to 'start again right from the foundations' is not a mere figure of speech. It is indeed the foundations of knowledge that he sets out to find in this inquiry.

Descartes' autobiographical sketch performs another task: of making the parameters of the inquiry apparent. His description of himself as 'here quite alone' is an indication of the kind of approach he will adopt. The inquiry will not be reliant on knowledge derived from others but will depend on what he can provide from his own resources. Further parameters become clear as Descartes continues:

To accomplish this, it will not be necessary for me to show that all my opinions are false, which is something I could perhaps never manage. Reason now leads me to think that I should hold back my assent from opinions which are not completely certain and indubitable just as carefully as I do from those which are patently false. (12)

The commitment to set aside all that is 'not completely certain and indubitable' sets the bar very high. This courts various problems, which we shall look into, but it has one great advantage: it makes the general strategy simplicity itself:

For the purpose of rejecting all my opinions, it will be enough if I find in each of them at least some reason for doubt. And to do this I will not need to run through them all individually, which would be an endless task. Once the foundations of a building are undermined, anything built on them collapses of its own accord; so I will go straight for the basic principles on which all my former beliefs rested. (12)

This autobiographical launch to the *Meditations* demonstrates Descartes' mastery of vigorous philosophical prose. He has the most enviable style of any philosopher: not just simple and clear and rigorous, but also enthralling and direct. This launch also marks out the particular way Descartes chooses to be a radical philosopher: he will take his stand on reason, particularly on reason-based reflection on his own current thoughts.

1. The nature of the inquiry

The opening passage of the *Meditations* gives us a clear sense of philosophy's role, as Descartes understood it. But why does Descartes set about things in this way? What exactly does he have in mind? What goals does he hope to secure by doing philosophy? To answer these questions, we need to look more closely at what stands behind the opening passage.

(i) Knowledge

Descartes' ultimate aim in the *Meditations* is to establish claims 'in the sciences'. Unlike many contemporaries who assumed that each science must have its own principles, he believes that the sciences form a unified system, that there are principles of knowledge which are general, applying to all sciences. Secure these principles, and the features peculiar to each science will have a proper underpinning.

Descartes thinks that the most basic general principles of knowledge are those given by an account of what knowledge is, in general, what we can know, in general, and how, in general, we are to go about acquiring knowledge – what we call a *theory* of knowledge. We would not look to any particular science to provide such a theory, in part because what we need is meant to be common to all the sciences, but mainly because it is not the aim of any particular science to come up with such a theory. Rather, the sciences tend to pursue their specific inquiries presupposing that we have a sufficient idea of what knowledge is, what we are capable of knowing and how we are to go about acquiring knowledge.

The one discipline whose task it is to provide a theory of knowledge is philosophy. And Descartes' claim here is that this inquiry, specific to philosophy, is a basic enterprise: the particular claims of the sciences will not be secure – will not be 'stable and likely to last' – unless and until they are grounded in a theory of knowledge. It is this claim that lies behind his plan 'to demolish everything completely and start again right from the foundations'. This is necessary 'to establish anything at all in the sciences' that might be stable and long-lasting.

(ii) Foundations

One striking feature about the opening passage is its dependence on building metaphors: 'the highly doubtful nature of the whole edifice'; 'to demolish everything completely and start again right from the foundations'; 'once the foundations of a building are undermined, anything built on them collapses of its own accord' (12).

What Descartes is alluding to here is the importance we place on connecting our beliefs to each other. Very often, it is because I believe one thing (e.g. that it is the sun which is streaming through my curtains) that I believe another (e.g. that the weather is good). Indeed, sometimes, believing that *p* can lead us to believe that *q* in such a way that, if I *know* that p and q, then I *know* that r. If I know that you are a human being, and I know that all human beings are mortal, then I know that you are mortal. In other words, beliefs can be interconnected in such a way as to be knowledge-advancing.

Descartes' key thought here is that, to be knowledge-advancing, beliefs must be connected to each other as the parts of a building are: with a superstructure dependent on foundations. My knowing that you are mortal, in the example, depends on my knowing that you are a human being, and my knowing this in turn depends on my knowing other things: what a human being is, for example, and what you are like. These pieces of knowledge are themselves dependent on knowing other things, and we could carry on tracing back these lines of dependence for an extended period. But in Descartes' view, if they really are pieces of knowledge, we will eventually come to the 'foundations' of this superstructure: to knowledge that does not itself depend on any deeper knowledge. Our beliefs must have such foundations to be knowledge-advancing.

It is because he believes this that Descartes is made so anxious by the suspicion he has false beliefs. It is not just 'the large number of falsehoods that I had accepted as true in my childhood' but 'the highly doubtful nature of the whole edifice that I had subsequently based on them'. And it is because he believes this that Descartes treats 'the general demolition of my opinions', which might otherwise seem like a very complex and exhausting endeavour, as not very demanding: 'Once the foundations of a building are undermined, anything built on them collapses of its own accord.' So this gives him a simple plan: to 'go straight for the basic principles on which all my former beliefs rested' (12).

(iii) Individualism

Another striking feature of the opening passage is that it is expressed throughout in the first person. The focus is on 'how can *I* establish claims in the sciences?', 'how can *I* find some reason to doubt?' and 'what are the basic principles on which *my* former beliefs rest?'

We might expect an inquiry into the basic principles of knowledge to approach matters in a more inclusive, universal way: 'how can one establish such claims?', 'what can be doubted?', 'what is the truth?', 'what can be known?' and so on. But this would allow the inquiry to take on the features of a communal or collective enterprise, one to which many might contribute. And Descartes is adamant that this would not be sufficient. To give himself the assurance he needs, it is not enough to be able to claim that the basic principles are known; he needs to be able to say 'I know them', where this means that he can justifiably assert his conclusions without depending on anyone else.

And this is to be the case for each of us who wishes to make this same inquiry for ourselves. This inquiry must be an individualistic one. To push home this point, Descartes takes the trouble to describe the isolated situation in which he settles down to pursue matters: 'I am here quite alone'; 'I have expressly rid my mind of all worries and arranged for myself a clear stretch of free time'; 'I will devote myself sincerely and without reservation to the general demolition of my opinions'.

(iv) High threshold

We cannot be said to *know* something if it is false. Knowledge is factive. Whatever we know must be true. But what more is required for something to count as knowledge? After all, there are very many truths that we do not know. What turns something from being a truth into something we know? Plausibly, the fact that we believe it, and that we have good reason to believe it, or, as we might also say, that we are justified in believing it.

But this would not be enough for Descartes. He insists that to know something, we must be completely certain of it, by which he means that there should be no room for doubt about it, that we should be in possession of information that serves utterly to rule out the hypothesis that what we take to be true is in fact false. This sets a very high standard indeed for something to count as knowledge. And it is because Descartes regards knowledge as 'high threshold' in this way that he proceeds as he does, setting aside much that he would otherwise regard himself as having good reason to believe, as being justified in believing. 'Reason now leads me to think that I should hold back my assent from opinions which are not completely certain and indubitable just as carefully as I do from those which are patently false.'

2. The sceptical situation

For Descartes, then, all inquiry depends on a philosophical search for individualistic certainty about the foundations of knowledge. And as his *Meditations* continue, he draws out the implications of this view. He is optimistic but guarded. He believes that truth is readily accessible to the ordinary human intellect, but only if that intellect is directed in the right way, so as to achieve individualistic certainty about the foundations of knowledge.

(i) Method of doubt

Descartes proceeds by adopting a method of doubt. We may summarize that method as follows: (1) Some of my beliefs are false and I have no way of telling which; so (2) I should undertake a review of all my beliefs and suspend them. (3) Taking my most fundamental beliefs first, I should reject those which fail to be completely certain and indubitable, as well as any which depend on them. (4) I will thus arrive at some claims of which I am certain. (5) I can thus build up from those claims to knowledge of the world.

It would be wrong to assume that this method depends on my supposing that *all* my beliefs are false. It is enough to suspend all my beliefs if I realize that, though some are false and some are true, I have no way of telling which is which. This is reasonable: if people with a nut allergy know that *some* of the cakes before them have been made with nuts, and if they have no way of telling these cakes apart from those *not* made with nuts, they should obviously avoid *all* the cakes. Moreover, it would be wrong to assume that this method aims at leaving one a sceptic. The scepticism is merely methodological, a technique one adopts for a particular purpose, one that may be discarded as soon as that purpose is achieved.

(ii) Descent into the sceptical situation

Descartes encourages us to review our beliefs in an ordered way, beginning with the testimony of the senses.

The senses have sometimes deceived us, so we should not trust them completely. He accepts that it would be mad to doubt our straightforward sense-based judgements – about non-tiny, non-distant objects for example. Nevertheless, if we are now dreaming, even straightforward sense-based judgements can be doubted. Again, he accepts that dreams are composed of objects from real life, so the world must contain such things as then appear. But he notes that items occurring in dreams may be as utterly imaginary and unreal as unicorns. Of course, even the most fictitious compositions have certain very simple and universal properties – their place in time and space, for example, their number and extension, size and shape. But he demonstrates that we may subtract every such property from a material object, being left only with spatial extension, so that none of the other properties 'really' belong to material objects. And as for arithmetic, God could make me go wrong every time I add 2 + 2. He acknowledges that there must then be a God, one who is perfect and therefore would not deceive us. But suppose there is no God. If neither our senses nor our reasoning faculty were created by God, one who is perfect, then there is even more reason to doubt them. Perhaps, even, there is an omnipotent deceiver, someone with the *intention* of deceiving us.

At this point – the end of his first *Meditation* – Descartes describes himself as in 'inextricable darkness'. He seems to know nothing at all about anything beyond him, and little if anything about himself either. It is his method of doubt that has brought him to this sceptical situation. But this method will also be the saving of him, as he will argue at the beginning of his second *Meditation*. Out of the very process of doubting everything comes *something* he does know. The darkness appears complete, but it is not in fact inextricable.

(iii) Methodological scepticism

Since doubt plays so significant a role in Descartes' inquiry, it is important to be clear about the kind of 'sceptic' Descartes is. It helps if we contrast his 'methodological scepticism' with the more ancient form of scepticism associated with Sextus Empiricus.

In Descartes' programme, I start in a state of pre-philosophical common sense. But then I am beset by doubts which develop out of resources that common sense can recognize as its own. This doubt clears my mind of prejudices that would blind me to new truths. And subsequent encounters with doubt lead me – with luck – to new certainties by which I overcome doubt. Hence, I attain a state of metaphysical enlightenment.

Sextus Empiricus also made doubt basic to his philosophizing (see his *Outlines of Pyrrhonism Bk. 1*). But his programme is very different. Here, I start in a state of peace of mind (*ataraxia*), which I prize more than anything. But this peace is disturbed by my awareness of various puzzles and paradoxes (e.g. Zeno's paradox; the Puzzle of the Heap), which put me in a state of doubt. So I look into matters for myself to determine the truth. My inquiries persuade me that one can argue with equal plausibility (*isosthenia*) for and against the claims at issue, and hence that these disputes are not resolvable. Thus, I come to make it my practice to suspend my judgement (*epoche*). And this, happily, returns me to peace of mind (*ataraxia*).

The main differences are these. Sextus Empiricus aims at suspension of judgement, whereas Descartes does not. Descartes aims at securing knowledge, and in particular knowledge of principles that can be used to secure further knowledge, whereas Sextus Empiricus does not. Sextus Empiricus is plunged by doubt into the sceptical situation, whereas Descartes uses doubt eventually to escape the sceptical situation.

3. Questions

We know something about what Descartes thought, and why, concerning the role of philosophy. We should now make a start at asking whether he was right. His plan was to 'start again', but doesn't the autobiographical sketch at the beginning of the *Meditations* assume much that is controversial? It may be that the game is already in play when we enter, and some of the principal pieces quite far advanced. If so, we may wonder whether Descartes is indeed offering us a genuinely open inquiry into the role of philosophy.

(i) Knowledge?

Descartes' notion that a theory of knowledge is basic depends partly on his belief that the sciences form a unified system. This is one assumption we may question. Descartes also seems to be assuming that nothing would count as knowledge in the sciences unless it was supported by a theory of knowledge. Spelling this out, what Descartes has in mind is that we need knowledge of a theory of knowledge in order to acquire knowledge in the sciences. But then we must ask how we can claim such knowledge. Do we need to have a theory of knowledge in order to acquire knowledge of a theory of knowledge? But then how could we ever acquire such knowledge? Or is the theory of knowledge something we acquire knowledge of without already having a theory of knowledge? But then why should this not apply to the sciences also; why do we need to have a theory of knowledge *there* in order to know things if we do not need it *here*? It may seem that Descartes exposes himself to another charge: treating philosophy as a kind of 'super-science', completely discontinuous from the sciences, with a subject-matter all its own and the right to dictate to each of the sciences on matters of peculiar concern to them. The passage may give this impression, but later discussions in the *Meditations* make clear that Descartes treated philosophy and the sciences as continuous with each other. If there is a broad distinction to be made, consistent with his view, it is that philosophy questions assumptions that the sciences must take for granted.

(ii) Foundations?

Descartes assumes that beliefs must be connected like parts of a building to be knowledge-advancing, with 'foundations' and 'superstructure'. But it might equally well be otherwise. The parts of a web are connected together, for example, but a web has no foundations. And it might be an advantage to conceive of knowledge-advancing connections without appeal to foundations, without requiring there to be some ultimate and fundamental set of beliefs that do not depend on anything but which nevertheless justify other beliefs. For if we ask how foundational beliefs are able to justify other beliefs, problems arise. We might say (a) some beliefs need no justification to be justifying. But it is hard to see how Descartes could be comfortable with this, given the reasons that prompt his inquiry, his sense that his initial situation lacks intellectual respectability. We might say (b) some beliefs are justified by something other than beliefs. But this is mysterious; what is this 'other' that justifies our beliefs? To appeal to something so enigmatic would not be consistent with the principles guiding Descartes' inquiry. Finally, we might say (c) some beliefs justify themselves. This is the option Descartes finds himself obliged to take. But this may seem limiting and not just mysterious. For suppose we accept this enigmatic category of beliefs that justify themselves. Such beliefs would surely be too rare and special to perform their foundational role of justifying *all* our other beliefs.

(iii) Individualism?

Descartes insists that a truly satisfying inquiry into the theory of knowledge must be thoroughly self-reflective and self-critical. One must have the resources not simply to say 'this is the case' but to be able justifiably to assert '*I* know this to be the case'. This seems to reflect his adoption of a very strong and perhaps unsustainable principle: that to know something, one must *know* that one knows it. Descartes also seems to move too swiftly in what he makes of his position here. Suppose one needs to be able justifiably to assert knowledge-claims in the first person. Descartes takes this to mean that one must rely exclusively on one's own resources, getting into this position by self-reflection alone, without depending on others. But this does not follow. The mere fact that one shares tasks with others does not undermine one's right to first-personal claims. Suppose one engages in a communal or collective inquiry that issues the group with the resources to be able to assert justifiably 'We know this to be the case'. So long as one can – subsequently if not immediately – recover these resources for oneself, there is no reason why this conclusion could not be asserted, equally justifiably, as '*I* know this to be the case'.

(iv) High threshold?

Descartes sets the bar for knowledge very high indeed. Knowledge is an achievement, and no doubt there is good reason to reject views that make success here too easily attainable. Nevertheless, we may regard Descartes' requirements as excessive. He insists that to know something, we must be absolutely certain of it, but we often distinguish the two, treating knowledge explicitly as easier to attain. (This is a conversation I overheard recently. A: 'Are you registered to vote?' B: 'Yes'. A: 'Do you know that?' B: 'Yes'. A: 'Are you *absolutely certain*?' B: 'Hmm, no . . .') And Descartes even sets a higher than usual bar for certainty. Ordinarily, we might say that if one has no room for doubt about something, one is certain of it. But Descartes insists that, to be certain, one must be in possession of information that serves utterly to rule out the hypothesis that what we take to be true is in fact false. Given that Descartes sets the bar so unusually high, it is a failing that he does not provide a supporting argument for his requirements on knowledge.

He also makes himself hostage to these requirements: many of his subsequent conclusions do not count as knowledge by these lights.

(v) Circularity?

Descartes' methodological scepticism uses doubt to deliver positive results. But there is a danger that he may be charged with circularity here. What gives us grounds to be suspicious is the fact that the positive results Descartes will achieve are so perfectly ordered to reflect his descent into the sceptical situation. Thus, his positive project starts with (a) beliefs that are never to be doubted, moves on to (b) beliefs about his origin, nature, and relation to providence, then (c) beliefs about things that are very simple and very general, then (d) beliefs about what his senses tell him concerning objects close by and in plain view, then (e) beliefs about what his senses tell him concerning objects generally. And this is a straightforward reversing of the initial negative project, which started with (e) and worked through the same ordering to (a).

Descartes' argument would be guilty of circularity if he somehow assumes the conclusion he arrives at in the very arguments meant to demonstrate that conclusion. One conclusion he means to demonstrate is that our beliefs must be ordered in a particular hierarchy to be knowledge-advancing, with the beliefs at (a) counting as the foundations, supporting the beliefs at (b), which in turn support the beliefs at (c) and so on. And what the perfect reflection between positive and negative projects seems to suggest is that he has already *assumed* that our beliefs must be so ordered when organizing his descent into the sceptical situation. The circularity then lies here: that he must *assume* that our beliefs are so ordered in order to *demonstrate* that our beliefs are so ordered.

(vi) Mere appearances?

In his descent into the sceptical situation, Descartes uses the possibility that he is then dreaming to doubt even his straightforward experience-based judgements. In doing so, he assumes that what we experience, even when we are not misled, is a mere appearance of the world rather than the world itself. If we agree, then we are conceiving our experience as essentially insulating us from the world itself, even when we are not misled. This is a threat we shall take up again in the next chapter.

We need not share Descartes' assumption here, which is another way of saying he owes us an argument. Clearly, we should agree with him that we sometimes dream, that what we experience in dream is mere appearance and that (often) we cannot tell whether we are waking or dreaming. But we need not agree that the fact we cannot tell implies that what we experience in dreaming is the same as what we experience when awake, that what we experience when we are awake is also mere appearance. The fact that we cannot tell is consistent with the possibility that what we experience is nevertheless different.

We might say, for example, that what we experience depends in part on what causes the experience; that what causes it in waking life (when we are not misled) is reality, whereas what causes it in dreaming is some complex goings-on in the brain; and hence that what we experience in waking life differs from what we experience in dreaming, despite the fact that we cannot tell. In this way, we can resist the idea that our experience is insulated from the world itself, even when we are not misled.

4. Possible paths to pursue

On the essential features of being radical in philosophy, it is helpful to consider a famous distinction P. F. Strawson makes between 'descriptive' and 'revisionary' metaphysics in *Individuals* (introduction), a characteristically close analysis of that distinction by Adrian Moore in *The Evolution of Modern Metaphysics: Making Sense of Things* (introduction), which brings out the significance of novelty and creativity, and the recent *Extremism: A Philosophical Analysis* by Quassim Cassam, a tour de force in conceptual geography which finds further reasons – befitting his wider scope – to place radicalism between conventionality on the one hand and extremism on the other.

Descartes published his *Meditations* alongside six sets of 'Objections' by various authors to which he then wrote 'Replies'. All these are usefully published together in the edition cited in the Bibliography.

Descartes by John Cottingham is an excellent guide to Descartes' philosophy, placing it squarely within its historical context while bringing out its contemporary resonance. For a close examination of Descartes' arguments concerning the right method for gaining knowledge, see Bernard Williams' *Descartes: The Project of Pure Inquiry* (chapter 2). For a detailed examination of Descartes' overall approach, see Janet Broughton's *Descartes' Method of Doubt*. Jonathan Dancy pursues the issues concerning knowledge through to the present in *An Introduction to Contemporary Epistemology* (chs 1–2, 4–5). On more specialist topics, see Stephen Gaukroger's *Descartes: An Intellectual Biography* for a thorough account of Descartes' scientific work and its influence on his philosophizing. For his place in the history of metaphysics, see Adrian Moore's *The Evolution of Modern Metaphysics* (introduction, chapter 1). For an individual but animated take on the way ideas about God influenced Descartes, see Edward Craig's *The Mind of God and the Works of Man* (chapter 1). An engaging introduction to the themes of ancient scepticism and the contemporary debates about it can be gained from five influential papers, now collected in *The Original Sceptics* (ed. Burnyeat and Frede). See also Michael Williams' article 'Descartes and the metaphysics of doubt', which draws the contrast with Sextus Empiricus and raises worries about what Descartes' progressive doubt assumes. For a celebrated account of forms of scepticism contemporary with Descartes, see Richard Popkin's *The History of Scepticism: From Erasmus to Spinoza*.

2

How we are

Descartes' *Meditations* is the book for which he is best known, but it was not his first publication. This was *Discourse on the Method*, which appeared anonymously at Leiden in 1637. It is a harder text to grapple with, so it was necessary to make a start before approaching it.

The *Discourse* is an astute blend of autobiography and philosophy and science. But it is nevertheless driven by a sense of urgency: to show off his method of rightly conducting reason so as to seek the truth in the sciences. Descartes called it a 'discourse' rather than a 'treatise' to show that he did not intend to teach the method but only to speak about it. His style is as simple and direct as in the *Meditations*. And precisely because Descartes wanted the *Discourse* to consist more in practice than in theory, it is as absorbing as the later work.

Philosophy can lead to mind-numbing doubt, to the fear that one knows nothing at all. Can philosophy also rescue one from this sceptical situation? Descartes thought so, and for reasons that mark him out as a particularly clear case of the radical. For him, the remedy is to immerse oneself as deeply as possible within the mind-numbing doubts that scepticism induces. He is convinced that engaging in this process will lead to truths about which we can be individualistically certain. And he thinks these truths will also serve as foundations for further knowledge.

This is radical in every sense: engaged with fundamental issues that matter to us all, and above all audacious. For what Descartes proposes is to make scepticism undermine itself, to use doubt to undermine doubt, to find truth and a foundation for knowledge in drinking the sceptic's bitter draught to its very dregs.

1. A thinking substance

The truth to which scepticism first leads Descartes is a truth about himself:

> observing that this truth 'I am thinking, therefore I exist' was so firm and sure that all the most extravagant suppositions of the sceptics were incapable of shaking it, I decided that I could accept it without scruple as the first principle of the philosophy I was seeking. (127; all page references in this chapter are to René Descartes' *Discourse on the Method*; see the Bibliography for full details.)

Descartes thinks this truth – 'I am thinking, therefore I exist' – can serve as the foundation for further knowledge. In particular, it helps show him what kind of thing he is. This 'I' which thinks is a substance, entirely distinct from and independent of everything else. Indeed, this substance is a thinking substance, independent of material things like the body and the brain.

The passages containing this argument are admirably clear, but the thought behind it could do with some teasing out. After all, it is not such a strange thing to suppose one is a thinking substance. How could that lead to the remarkably counter-intuitive idea that this substance is entirely distinct from the body? We shall follow Descartes' line of thought as he pursues it in a dense passage of the *Discourse*.

(i) 'I am thinking, therefore I exist'

Descartes, we know, assumes that a philosophical inquiry must take a certain form if it is to meet his ultimate goal, to establish claims in the sciences. His insight is that immersion in the sceptical situation allows inquiry to take this form. So although the truths thus revealed are indubitable, there is an important sense in which they are not 'beyond doubt'.

> But immediately I noticed that while I was endeavouring in this way to think that everything was false, it was necessary that I, who

> was thinking this, was something. And observing that this truth 'I
> am thinking, therefore I exist' was so firm and sure that all the most
> extravagant suppositions of the sceptics were incapable of shaking it,
> I decided that I could accept it without scruple as the first principle of
> the philosophy I was seeking. (127)

How does this approach enable Descartes to satisfy his own
requirements? First, it enables him to proceed individualistically,
without reliance on anyone else. His own doubts and his own reasoning
about them are sufficient for him to acquire the knowledge he claims,
his 'first principle': 'I am thinking, therefore I exist'. Second, this
knowledge is high threshold, certain and indubitable. The very process
of doubting confirms to his own satisfaction that he is thinking, utterly
ruling out the hypothesis that what he then believes ('I exist') is false.
Third, this approach provides him with a foundation, a 'first principle',
thus meeting his requirement for beliefs if they are to be knowledge-
advancing. Finally, these three previous gains enable him to meet the
fourth requirement of philosophical inquiry. By providing him with a
method for acquiring and assessing beliefs, together with the assurance
that this method will enable him to acquire further knowledge,
Descartes makes the theory of knowledge basic. His way of facing up to
the sceptical situation ensures this.

(ii) I cannot pretend I do not exist, but I can pretend everything else does not exist

> Next I examined attentively what I was. I saw that while I could pretend
> that I had no body and that there was no world and no place for me to
> be in, I could not for all that pretend that I did not exist. (127)

Descartes draws conclusions about himself from the conjunction of the
sceptical situation with his newly minted 'first principle'. The reasoning
here is condensed, but he seems to be offering two different but
mutually supportive arguments to two related but notionally distinct
conclusions.

One argument depends on considerations about *doubting*. Descartes enters into the depths of the sceptical situation by supposing that what he thinks and experiences is under the control of an omnipotent deceiver, out to deceive him in every possible way. On the one hand, he may then doubt almost everything (we are evidently to treat what he lists here as shorthand for all he has shown himself able to doubt): that he has a body, that there is a world or any place for him to be in, that he has a past, that anyone or indeed anything else exists and so on. On the other hand, even (or rather especially) in this situation, what he cannot doubt is that he himself exists.

(iii) If I cease thinking, I have no reason to believe I exist

Descartes' second argument concerning himself depends on considerations about *not thinking*:

> I saw on the contrary that from the mere fact that I thought of doubting the truth of other things, it followed quite evidently and certainly that I existed; whereas if I had merely ceased thinking, even if everything else I had ever imagined had been true, I should have had no reason to believe that I existed. (127)

Descartes is again reflecting on the conjunction of the first principle and the sceptical situation. He notes that he was able to acquire reason to believe this truth, that he exists, from a 'mere fact' about this situation: 'that I thought of doubting the truth of other things'. And what he now recognizes is that he would have been unable to acquire such reason if just one element of that situation were different: namely, 'if I had merely ceased thinking'.

(iv) I am a certain sort of thinking substance

Descartes now draws two conclusions about himself from these two mutually supportive arguments. He takes the first (from doubt) to show that, whatever he is, it must be something independent of any body, any world or place, any past, any one or indeed any other thing. And he takes the second (from not thinking) to show that it is just one element – thinking, and nothing but thinking – that is essential to him.

> From this I knew I was a substance whose whole essence or nature is solely to think, and which does not require any place, or depend on any material thing, in order to exist. (127)

Given these considerations, Descartes concludes that his existence and identity are entirely distinct from and independent of anything else:

> Accordingly this 'I' – that is, the soul by which I am what I am – is entirely distinct from the body, and indeed it is easier to know than the body, and would not fail to be whatever it is, even if the body did not exist. (127)

Clarifying what he takes himself to have shown, Descartes uses the phrase 'this "I"', by which he means the thing to which the 'I' of his first principle refers, that whose existence cannot be doubted. He particularly emphasizes one aspect of the independence of this 'I', presumably because it is the most surprising: that it is 'entirely distinct' from the body (his own body, that is).

For Descartes, the referent of 'I' is a substance, something which exists independently. Furthermore, he treats this substance as a thinking substance, and in a particularly strong sense: thinking is essential to its existence, and nothing but thinking is essential to its existence. In later work, he uses his knowledge that he is a thinking substance to validate his sense-based beliefs about the external world and thus complete his remedy for the sceptical situation. But whether this is indeed a remedy depends on the quality of its foundations. So it is worth looking again at Descartes' claims regarding his own nature as a thinking substance.

2. Questions

Descartes' audacious response to the sceptical situation is to immerse himself in doubt. The sceptical situation is then supposed to undermine itself, doubt leading to knowledge of a truth that can ground further knowledge. But we may wonder about Descartes' optimism here. Immersion in doubt may lead him to individualistic certainty that 'I am thinking' and 'I exist'. But does he succeed in making these claims the foundation of knowledge?

One worry we shall have concerns Descartes' subsequent arguments. Does he establish his claims about himself, the thinking substance he takes himself to be? Deeper worries arise if we allow him these claims. Do they not serve to undermine his own position? For suppose that his existence and identity are entirely distinct from and independent of anything else. This claim threatens to insulate the thinking substance from the rest of the world. If so, Descartes' claims about what he is may simply plunge him more deeply into the sceptical situation.

(i) What do I know about this 'I'?

'I' is a referring expression, something that picks out and refers to a 'something'. But given what Descartes is supposed to be methodically doubting away, he should presumably also doubt that there is such a thing for him to refer to. If he does not, doubting will not deliver his required high-threshold individualistic certainty about the claims 'I am thinking' and 'I exist'. This may be the point behind a famous but gnomic remark by Lichtenberg. We can put the point differently. The activity of doubting may rule out the hypothesis that it is false to suppose that there is thinking going on, but it does not seem to rule out the hypothesis that it is false to suppose there is a thinker, a 'something' responsible for doing this thinking, a referent for 'I' in phrases of the form 'I am thinking' and 'I exist'. Descartes' way of phrasing his argument may appear to answer this point – 'while I was endeavouring in this way to think that everything was false, it was necessary that I, who was thinking this, was something' – but only by courting circularity. For if he can rule out the hypothesis that it is false to suppose there is an 'I' who is thinking these doubt-thoughts, then he is certainly in a position to assert that 'I am something'; but he can only rule out this hypothesis if he has already gained the right to use the referring term 'I', something that can only be used successfully if there is indeed a referent for the use, and this would mean that he is already in a position to assert 'I am something'.

(ii) What can I doubt?

Descartes claims that he cannot doubt he himself ('I') exists, and that he can doubt anything else exists. The first claim amounts to very little. Even if we accept it, little may follow – indeed, perhaps considerably less than Descartes may later require. For what is this 'I' whose existence he cannot doubt? Nothing material, evidently, and nothing in the past, because the act of doubting does not rule out the hypothesis that he is immaterial and has no past. If we grant him his essentially formal assumption that there must be a thinker for thinking to be going on, then there is a 'something' whose existence cannot be doubted. But it is only a very thin something: nothing more than the thinker of this very thought, something whose existence cannot be assumed to reach beyond this present moment and whose features cannot be assumed to extend beyond this particular mental act. Endow this formal present-bound dot with any such dimensions, and it will not pass Descartes' high threshold test: he *could* pretend that it does not exist because the hypothesis that it does not exist could not be ruled out as false.

Descartes' second claim, that he can doubt anything else exists, is vulnerable to a different sort of pressure. Is it really possible to pretend that one has no body, no material form? Close your eyes, and let your imagination loose. It is easy to pretend you have a *different* material form; but that is not the trick. It is also easy to imagine *something* without material form; but that is not the trick either. What you have to pretend is that this *something* without material form is *you*. And that proves very difficult indeed. (It may be that Descartes makes things unnecessarily difficult for himself here. Being able to pretend that something is not the case differs from being able to doubt that it is the case. For example, perhaps I can *doubt* I have material form without being able to take on successfully the imaginative project of *pretending* I have none. Although Descartes does formulate his argument in terms of the ability to pretend, he only really needs the ability to doubt.)

(iii) What if I cease thinking?

Descartes takes himself to have had no reason to believe he existed until he had proved it to himself beyond any possibility of doubt. But why should we agree? Often enough we think the simple fact that something is true gives one reason to believe it. (Whether we ever *do* believe what we have reason to believe is another matter, of course; just as whether or not we ever perform some act may be quite distinct from whether we have reason to perform it.) Admittedly, we do sometimes restrict the phrase 'reason to believe' to cases where we have considered the possibility that something is true and have something that counts as evidence for it. (If we think there is something odd about saying 'we have reason to believe there is a little green man at the end of the universe' when we haven't even considered the possibility and certainly have no evidence for it, it is presumably because we have this sense in mind). But Descartes' sense is considerably more restrictive even than this and in a way that seems quite implausible. I do not need to have proved it to myself beyond all possibility of doubt that my belly will need food soon in order to have reason to believe it; the length of time since my last meal and these characteristic discomforts are sufficient.

(iv) Must I be a certain sort of thinking substance?

Descartes, recall, derives different parts of this claim from different considerations – about *doubting* and about *not thinking*. We should take each in turn.

(a) Doubting

Descartes thinks that, whatever he is, it must be something independent of any body, any world or place, any past, any one or indeed any other thing. His argument is essentially this: (1) I can pretend that my body (etc.) does not exist; but (2) I cannot pretend that I do not exist; so (3) I must be independent of my body (etc.). If this were a valid argument, it would be inconsistent to assert (1) and (2) while denying (3). Indeed, if the argument is valid, it would be inconsistent more generally to assert (1) I can pretend that A is not F and (2) I cannot pretend that B is not F, while denying (3) A must be independent of B. But to see that something is going wrong here, let us give different values for 'A', 'B' and 'is F'. In Descartes' argument, 'A' stands for 'my body', 'B' for 'I' and 'is F' for 'has the property of existing'. Suppose instead that 'A' stands for 'Archibald Leach', 'B' for 'Cary Grant' and 'is F' for 'has the property of being Cary Grant'. Then we have (1) I can pretend that Archibald Leach does not have the property of being Cary Grant, (2) I cannot pretend that Cary Grant does not have the property of being Cary Grant and (3) Archibald Leach must be independent of Cary Grant. Now it is perfectly possible (and is historically true) that Cary Grant and Archibald Leach are the same person and hence not independent of each other. So we have to accept that it would *not* be inconsistent to assert (1) and (2) while denying (3). Hence, it would *not* be valid to argue from (1) and (2) to (3). The same goes for Descartes' argument because it shares the same form, and validity is a matter of form.

(b) Not thinking

Descartes thinks that there is just one feature – thinking, and nothing but thinking – that is essential to him. His argument here is very condensed, and it is not easy to be confident about what he has in mind. But it does seem that we can break the chain of reasoning and that no replacement link will do what is required of it.

It seems that Descartes is arguing as follows: (i) given my doubting, I know I am thinking; thus (ii) I know I exist; and thus (iii) if I cease thinking, then I have no reason to believe I exist; hence (iv) I am a substance whose essence is thinking alone. But evidently (iv) does not follow from (iii). (iii) is consistent with the negation of (iv). Suppose my essence is thinking plus an extra feature 'F'. It might still be the case that I have no reason to believe I exist if I cease thinking (i.e. 'F' can be essential to me without helping in this regard).

We might strengthen (iii) considerably so that it is instead (iii*) 'If I cease thinking, then I do not exist'. But even this will not entail (iv). (iii*) may make thinking *necessary* for my existence, but what (iv) requires is that thinking be both *sufficient* and necessary for my existence. Furthermore, we have as yet no reason to believe (iii*). It certainly does not follow from (i) and (ii), since (i) and (ii) are obviously consistent with the negation of (iii*).

3. Trojan Horse syndrome

The Trojans brought about their own destruction by drawing their enemies – contained in the wooden horse – into the heart of their city. Philosophers are vulnerable to the same problem when they draw claims into the heart of their position which undermine that position. Descartes may be in danger of doing this.

Having established truths about which he can be individualistically certain, Descartes encounters difficulties, as we have seen. His arguments may fail to establish his claims about the thinking substance he takes himself to be. And this means that he has no secure foundation for his subsequent claims. But there is a deeper worry, which has to do with Descartes' audacity, his attempt to make scepticism undermine itself, to remedy the sceptical situation by immersing himself in doubt.

Descartes claims that his existence and identity are entirely distinct from and independent of anything else. And the deeper problem is not whether he *demonstrates* this claim but simply that he makes it and insists on making it. For if the claim were true, it looks as if this might undermine the possibility of his relating to the world, and hence plunge him more deeply into the sceptical situation. And this would be so despite his avowed purpose, the explicit design laid out in his subsequent *Meditations*, which is to overcome that situation. That is how Descartes may be like the Trojans, who drew the wooden horse into their own city. By drawing his claim into the heart of his project, he risks undermining it completely.

(i) Insulation

Recall what Descartes proves to his own satisfaction: that he is a substance whose essence is thinking and nothing but thinking, that this thinking substance is completely distinct from and easier to know than anything material and that it needs nothing material – neither a body nor a place – for its existence (i.e. to exist at all) or for its identity (i.e. to exist in the way it exists, 'to be whatever it is'). For suppose we agree that this thinking substance is indeed entirely independent so that it could have its thoughts and experiences *whether or not* the world exists and (if it does exist) *however* the world is. Then it is difficult to see how this thinking substance could be said to relate to the world – to think *about* the world and, conversely, to be impinged on *by* the world in experience. For to say that a thinking substance relates to the world in these ways is to say that it is exposed to the world and capable of being affected by it, that it would not have precisely these thoughts, these experiences, unless the world existed and in this particular way. In short, Descartes seems to preclude the kind of exposure required if the thinking substance is to relate to the world.

Not that Descartes need be regarded as wholly detaching the thinking substance from the world, cutting it off from the world altogether. But in depicting the thinking substance as shielded from exposure to the world, as protected from being affected by the world – in *insulating* it from the world, for short – he does seem to undermine the possibility of its being related to the world in the ways required for its thoughts to be *about* the world, for its experiences to be experiences *of* the world. And if the thinking substance is not related to the world in these ways, then it can know nothing about it.

So Descartes' remedy for the sceptical situation actually plunges us back into it. Being insulated, we know nothing at all about anything beyond us, and little if anything about ourselves either. This is the Trojan Horse syndrome, as it arises for Descartes.

(ii) Insulation and knowledge

One consequence of Descartes' insulation relates to knowledge. If I could have exactly the same thoughts and experiences that I do have, whether or not the world exists, can I really be said to know the world exists at all, let alone that it is as I experience it as being?

This knowledge problem is of particular interest given the sceptical situation that Descartes faces and seeks to remedy. But the logical gulf between mind and world threatened by Descartes' views on his nature goes much deeper than a knowledge problem. My ability to know about the world may be compromised without depriving me of the ability to *think* about the world, to *experience* it. Obviously so. After all, I can think about things in the world and be wrong about them. In these respects, I am a thinker without being a knower. In a similar way, I can be an experiencer without being a knower – when I am subject to illusions, for example, I have experiences of the world, but they misrepresent the way things actually are. And it is these deeper possibilities which Descartes' views threaten, not just my ability to know the world. If he is right about his own nature, it is hard to see how he could even be thinking about or experiencing the world, let alone being right or wrong about it, let alone being knowledgeable about it.

(iii) Insulation and dualism

This insulation of the mind might be confused with another claim, which Descartes is notorious for advocating: Substance Dualism. This is the idea that there are only two ultimate classes of things, thinking things and material things. But insulation is really quite different from Substance Dualism. Indeed, one might advocate either claim while rejecting the other. So philosopher X might be committed to the idea that there are two ultimate classes of things, mental and material, but nevertheless insist that our thoughts and experiences are such that, at least on occasion, they are dependent for their existence and identity on the world (one would not have had precisely *this* thought or *that* experience then, unless the world existed, and existed in some particular way). Conversely, philosopher Y might be committed to the idea that there is just one ultimate class of things, consisting wholly of material things say, and yet insist that the group of material things called 'my mind' or 'my thoughts' or 'my experiences' could exist, just as they are, whether or not, and however, the rest of the material world existed.

It is important to keep insulation separate from Substance Dualism. This is partly because the latter is so frequently regarded as untenable. If Dualism is confused with insulation, it might wrongly be assumed that no additional argument is necessary to reject insulation. Another danger in not separating them is that problems particular to insulation will not come to the fore. We can imagine anti-dualist philosophers supposing they have thrown off all vestiges of 'Cartesianism' who nevertheless enmesh themselves in materialist versions of Descartes' insulation.

4. Possible paths to pursue

John Cottingham offers a useful introduction to the specific topics discussed in this chapter in *Descartes* (chs 3–6). Older but still insightful accounts can be found in Anthony Kenny's *Descartes: A Study of His Philosophy*, Bernard Williams' *Descartes: The Project of Pure Inquiry* (chs 3–4, 10) and Margaret Wilson's *Descartes*. For the scientific context, see Stephen Gaukroger's *Descartes: An Intellectual Biography*. For more recent investigations, see Marleen Rozemond's *Descartes' Dualism* and Lilli Alanen's *Descartes's Concept of Mind*. John Heil's *Philosophy of Mind* (chapter 2) has a useful account of Descartes' broader legacy in philosophy of mind. The classic attempt to evacuate Descartes' ideas from the way we philosophize about the mind is *The Concept of Mind* by Gilbert Ryle. Chapter 1 gives the flavour, but one must read the whole for the full dose. For a more recent and measured attempt to do away with Descartes' approach to the mind, see Anthony Kenny's *The Metaphysics of Mind*. John Foster makes a vigorous attempt to rescue Descartes-like views about the mind and the self in *The Immaterial Self*. For an overview of dualism, in its many varieties, see Howard Robinson's 'Dualism'.

Radical II

Experience

3

How we know

John Locke (1632–1704) published his *Essay Concerning Human Understanding* in 1690 when he was nearly sixty years old. He had worked on it for twenty years. The claims are bold and the prose style elaborate and sophisticated, so the book deserved its immediate and admiring audience. Generations later, Laurence Sterne could still count on a sufficient knowledge of the *Essay* to satirize its style and central themes in his comic novel *Tristram Shandy* (1759).

Locke differs greatly from Descartes in his ideas about philosophy's role and what it shows. He is just as much a radical, audacious about his engagement with issues that are fundamental and matter to us all – recall that it is the combination of all these elements that is crucial to radical philosophy. And he is almost as optimistic. But he takes his stand on experience rather than on reasoned reflection on his own current thoughts.

He thinks we know a good deal already, and with complete certainty. We know with certainty, for example, that there are things of which we have experience, that some of these things are solid and three-dimensional objects and that some of them are thinking beings. This level of knowledge is simply inescapable for us. Hence the sceptical situation – where we know nothing at all about anything beyond us, and little if anything about ourselves either – is simply not a live possibility for us. So Locke sees no need, indeed no real possibility, of immersing oneself in doubt in the manner approved by Descartes. But Locke's optimistic audacity about fundamental matters is not unbounded. He sets strict limits to the knowledge it is possible to acquire. We know there *are* solid, three-dimensional substances, but we know little or nothing about *how* they are, about their underlying nature.

The passage we shall examine closely is typical Locke: dense with metaphor, sophisticated and elaborate, never repeating a verb when another can vary the tone. But this constant modulation, which makes reading Locke so pleasant, also allows ambiguities to thrive. Does Locke's varied style reflect a certain variability in his own mind, an undecidedness about his own position that underlies the surface confidence? Perhaps. This presents commentators with lively challenges. But we shall largely pass over the controversies, issuing only this warning: what follows is a plausible interpretation, no more; it is certainly not the only interpretation available.

1. Knowing substances

Locke defines knowledge as the perception of 'ideas', where what he means by ideas are contents of the mind that represent things. When I think 'That apple before me is ripe', for example, part of what is going on is that I have such an idea in my mind, an idea that is of or about this particular apple. As a thinker, I combine this idea with others to compose this particular thought.

For Locke, ideas are quite different from ordinary objects, like apples. First, you and I can share an apple but not an idea. My idea could *only* be mine. This makes ideas *logically private*. Second, an apple continues to exist if no one has it, but not an idea. An idea exists only if it is being thought or entertained. This makes ideas *thinking-dependent*. If we put these two points together, Locke's ideas resemble headaches: you cannot have mine, and mine do not exist unless I am feeling them.

Locke's ideas appear in the mind via experience and the five 'outer' senses ('sensation') and then become available to the 'inner' sense ('reflection'). He regards their ultimate source as experience and treats experience as that in which all knowledge is grounded. This position makes Locke an 'empiricist'. It distinguishes him markedly from Descartes, who grounded knowledge in reason, in rational reflection on his own current thoughts.

(i) Knowing there are substances

Locke draws conclusions from these claims about ideas and knowledge. When he is thinking, he knows with certainty that he is thinking. So he knows that he has ideas. And he would be unable to think at all unless experience of things had provided him with these ideas. So he knows with equal certainty that there are things of which he has experience.

This is a considerable claim and one we ought to investigate further. Locke argues first that experience gives him a certain amount of indubitable knowledge about substances, knowledge that can be distinguished by its source and by its product:

> Sensation convinces us, that there are solid extended Substances; and Reflection, that there are thinking ones. (312; all page references in this chapter are to John Locke's *An Essay Concerning Human*; see the Bibliography for full details)

Furthermore, he claims that the ideas which experience gives him are 'clear' in some respects; so much so that he knows equally indubitably that these kinds of substance have the following defining characteristics:

> Experience assures us of the Existence of such Beings; and that the one hath a power to move Body by impulse, the other by thought; this we cannot doubt of. Experience, I say, every moment furnishes us with the clear Ideas, both of the one, and the other. (312)

The first kind of power is that exhibited by a billiard ball when it hits another and thus causes it to move. The second kind of power is that exhibited by a player when she moves to recover the ball; she goes through a mental process (a 'thought' which Locke identifies with willing) that causes her body to move.

(ii) Knowing the nature of substances

Locke then imposes constraints on what it is possible to know. These constraints also follow directly from his empiricism and his notion of what ideas are:

> But beyond these Ideas, as received from their proper sources, our Faculties will not reach. (312)

The 'proper sources' of the ideas of sensation and reflection, no matter how complex, are ultimately the same: experience. And there is much we do not experience, or at least do not 'perceive clearly' – for example, the 'nature' of solid objects and thinking beings, conceived as something that stands behind and explains the way in which such objects and beings manifest themselves:

> If we could enquire farther into their Nature, Causes, and Manner, we perceive not the Nature of Extension, clearer than we do of Thinking. If we would explain them any farther, one is as easy as the other; and there is no more difficulty, to conceive how a Substance we know not, should by thought set Body into motion, than how a Substance we know not, should by impulse set Body into motion. So that we are no more able to discover, wherein the Ideas belonging to Body consist, than those belonging to Spirit. (312)

Though we know indubitably *that* there are substances, and though we are capable of knowing much about the way substances *manifest* themselves (e.g. what they look or sound like; what they are able to do), we are unable to know what stands behind these manifestations, what causes them, what explains them. And from this Locke infers that, although we do have ideas of solid objects and thinking beings, we are unable to know the 'nature' of substances.

(iii) Boundaries of thought

Locke infers something else from these limitations on our 'faculties':

> From whence it seems probable to me, that the simple Ideas we receive from Sensation and Reflection, are the Boundaries of our Thoughts;

beyond which, the Mind, whatever efforts it would make, is not able
to advance one jot; nor can it make any discoveries, when it would pry
into the Nature and hidden Causes of those Ideas. (312)

Locke's prose makes this conclusion seem smooth and inevitable. But
consider how radical it is, how audacious. It is not just that we are
unable to *know* anything beyond the clear perceptions characteristic
of 'simple' ideas. Locke studiedly describes these ideas as forming the
boundaries of our *thoughts*. So, on his view, it is impossible to *think*
beyond these simple ideas gained in experience.

We may have assumed otherwise. Indeed, that is precisely what
Descartes did assume. He took himself to be able to think and know –
independently of the experience he discounted as fallible – that he was
doubting, thinking, existing. But to do this would simply be to court
illusion, on Locke's view.

So Locke professes a limited optimism. We start out from a position
that would satisfy even Descartes' high-threshold requirement for
knowledge. We can be individualistically certain that there are solid,
three-dimensional objects and thinking beings, each with powers to
move other objects. Equally, however, we have to accept that there is
much we cannot know. The nature of such substances is his example
of this deficiency. And we also have to recognize that, no matter what
Descartes and others may suppose, it is simply not possible for us to
think beyond our simple ideas.

2. Philosophy's role

Locke's empiricism makes experience the ultimate source of knowledge.
Science is the systematic investigation of experience. So it is natural
for him to identify science with that which provides the principles on
which knowledge is based. Hence he does not agree with Descartes
that the theory of knowledge is truly foundational. Indeed, he denies
that any form of philosophy could fulfil that role. The task he gives
philosophy is much humbler, that of 'underlabourer' to science. It clears

up confusions in the path of scientific progress. It clarifies the meaning of terms, for example, and identifies mistakes in reasoning (fallacies) which render arguments invalid.

These differences between Locke and Descartes bring others in their train. Locke does not insist on a high threshold for knowledge (though his claims about substances satisfy it, as we have seen). We can often rely on what seems highly probable, rather than on what is indubitable. Again, he does not require that knowledge be individualistic (though again his claims about substances satisfy it). We can rely on what others have demonstrated. These differences mean that Locke's position squares much more easily with science than Descartes' position – for science cannot require the certainty of deductive validity. The high probability of a good inductive argument is in general all that it can hope for. And science cannot require individualism. It is a communal endeavour whose progress in any one area depends on deference to what experts in other areas have been able to demonstrate to their own satisfaction.

Whether Locke's response to the sceptical situation succeeds depends on his grounding claims. It is particularly important to look into Locke's argument for empiricism and to examine his claims about the ideas which experience gives him, ideas which make knowledge possible, but also constrain knowledge in the ways we have seen characterize his position.

(i) Experience

Locke claims that, if we do know something, it is by appeal (at least ultimately) to experience. This empiricism needs arguments in its favour because it is certainly not just obviously true.

For one thing, we know that it is possible to reject it for reasons that seem plausible enough. Descartes provides some, as we have seen. For another, there do seem to be things we know without having to appeal to experience. This might be said, for example, of certain truths of mathematics (like '7 + 5 = 12'), of certain truths about concepts and the meaning of words (like 'all aunts are female') and of certain truths of logic and reasoning (like 'nothing can both have and not have some particular property F', the so-called law of non-contradiction). Is it really plausible to insist that one's claim to know these truths stands in need of an appeal to *experience*? (It would be some sort of joke to say 'Well, I've never seen 7 and 5 add up to anything other than 12' or 'So far, at any rate, I've not met any non-female aunts'.)

These kinds of problem are the subject of much discussion by Locke. To answer them, he offers the following argument. If there is something that we know *without* making ultimate appeal to experience, it must be given us prior to any experience. It must be something we are born with, hence something innate. And if something we know is innate, it must be universally known. For it would not be coherent or plausible to suppose that some are born with knowledge prior to any experience that others are not similarly born with. But, so Locke claims, nothing is universally known. So it follows that there is nothing we know which is innate. Hence there is nothing that we know without having appeal to experience. And this is as much as to say that, if we do know something – even those truths of mathematics, meaning and logic which caused our problems – it must be by making ultimate appeal to experience.

3. Questions

Armed with his empiricism, Locke thinks there is much that we cannot help but know about the world and ourselves. But it may be that his confidence is misplaced. Is it really the case that we can refuse to treat the sceptical situation as a threat?

One issue we may raise is whether we do *know* that there are solid, three-dimensional objects and thinking beings, each with powers to move other objects. Another issue is whether these substances have natures that we *cannot* know. A third is whether it is indeed impossible for us to think beyond the simple ideas of sensation and reflection. And a fourth is whether Locke really does offer us good reason to adopt his empiricism. But underlying these relatively narrow issues, there is a much bigger and more general problem.

This problem arises from Locke's position, that we cannot think beyond the simple ideas of sensation and reflection, ideas that are logically private and thinking dependent. For reasons we shall come to, this claim may block the possibility of our ever acquiring any knowledge about the world at all. If so, wouldn't this claim fatally undermine Locke's philosophizing, whose whole purpose is to clear a path for the acquisition of knowledge about the world by science?

(i) What can we know indubitably?

Locke claims 'we cannot doubt of' the fact that there are thinking substances with the power to move bodies by thought. But his considerations seem no more robust than those of Descartes.

It may be indubitable, in certain circumstances, that there is thinking going on. But this does not rule out the hypothesis that it is false to suppose there is a thinker, a 'substance' responsible for doing this thinking, a referent for 'I' in phrases of the form 'I am thinking' and 'I exist'. And if the existence of thinking substances is something we may doubt, then so is the existence of thinking substances that move bodies by thought. Moreover, it is not beyond doubt that bodies exist, let alone that they are subject to being moved.

Locke also claims 'we cannot doubt of' the fact that there are solid and extended substances with the power to move bodies by impulse. But the empiricism he deploys here seems to stop well short of what he needs. If he knows indubitably that thinking is going on and that any such thinking employs ideas that must ultimately derive from experience of 'things', then it is perhaps indubitable that there are 'things'. But this does not rule out the hypothesis that it is false to suppose that such 'things' are solid and extended substances, let alone that they have the power to move other bodies by impulse. The ideas given us by experience certainly *present* the world as containing solid, extended substances with such powers. But we may very well doubt whether this is in fact how the world *is*.

(ii) What is it impossible to know?

Locke claims it is impossible to know the nature of substances. But why suppose substances *have* a nature, that there is something 'there' that we cannot know? And is Locke not overstepping the very boundaries he is trying to impose in assuming there is something 'there'?

Suppose we accept that our faculties will not reach further than the manifestations of substances. Then we do not – presumably *could* not – have reason to believe that substances have a 'nature', conceived as that which stands behind such manifestations, causing and explaining them.

Reversing direction, we may also question the boundary Locke imposes here. Suppose we accept his claim that we do not 'perceive . . . clearer' the nature of solid objects than the nature of thinking beings. Why require that something be perceived clearly to be knowable? Indeed, why require that it be perceived at all? We know things that are not themselves experienced but can be inferred from what we do experience; this seems perfectly compatible with empiricism.

(iii) Is it impossible to think beyond simple ideas?

Locke is dealing here with what 'seems probable' rather than with what is beyond doubt. Still, his claim seems far more radical than the evidence in its support. If it is compatible with empiricism to accept that we know things that go beyond what we directly experience, then we can know things beyond the simple ideas of sensation and reflection. And the boundaries on what we can know are more restrictive than those on what we can think – hence the possibility of thinking things that are not true and believing true things that we are not justified in believing. So, even from an empiricist standpoint, we may ask whether it does indeed 'seem probable' that we cannot think beyond the simple ideas of sensation and reflection.

4. Trojan Horse syndrome

Descartes faced the Trojan Horse syndrome because he drew claims into the heart of his position which undermine that position. It may be that Locke manifests a similarly systematic self-undermining tendency.

Having established his empiricism, Locke faces difficulties as we have seen. His arguments for a limited optimism about our knowledge of substances do not seem cogent. But these weaknesses may not be the most significant flaws in his system. At worst, they mean that he cannot simply shrug off the threat of the sceptical situation, that he has to treat it as a live possibility unless and until he comes up with cogent arguments to show that in fact we can and do know much about things beyond us.

But there is a deeper worry, and it has to do with Locke's audacity, his attempt to set limits to thought. This attempt obliges him to treat the sceptical situation not only as a live possibility but also as the *actual* situation. And this is a major flaw, given that his avowed purpose is to clear a way for science and its knowledge-enriching investigation of the world.

The explanation for this flaw lies not in what Locke fails to *show* but in what he *claims* and insists on: that we cannot think beyond the simple ideas of sensation and reflection, conceived as logically private and thinking-dependent contents of the mind. For this claim threatens to detach the mind from the world so that the sceptical situation becomes actual: we really do know nothing at all about anything beyond us, and little about ourselves. And since it is Locke's own views that preclude the possibility of our relating to the world in the ways required for scientific progress, his philosophizing undermines its own aims. His system is self-defeating.

(i) Detachment

Recall the position Locke takes up here: that our thoughts are composed of ideas, conceived as representing contents of our minds; that these contents are quite different in kind from ordinary objects:

like headaches, they are logically private (I can only have mine; I cannot share yours, and you cannot share mine), and they are thinking dependent (mine exist just in case I am thinking them – entertaining this idea is like feeling this headache; neither exists if I am not 'thinking' them); and that it is impossible even to think – let alone know – anything beyond certain ideas, namely the simple ones given us by sensation and reflection.

Now when we say that we think or know things about the world beyond us – when we think 'this apple is ripe', for example – we mean precisely that we think or know *about* things beyond us, that our thoughts reach beyond the contents of our own minds to ordinary objects, that we are capable of thinking beyond the peculiar and distinct kinds of item that ideas are, that the objects we relate to in thought include the kinds of item that apples are: objects that can be shared (i.e. not logically private) and that can exist when they are not being thought (i.e. not thinking dependent).

So Locke's claims about the nature and limits of thought seem to *detach* the mind from the world and thus preclude the kind of relations required if we are even to think – let alone know – things about the world beyond us. Our ability to think and to know is limited to the contents of our own minds, to items that we cannot share with others and which exist only so long as, and in so far as, they are being thought.

If we are of such a kind as to be incapable of thinking beyond our own simple ideas, conceived as logically private and thinking-dependent items, it is difficult to see how Locke could maintain, cogently and without self-contradiction, that our minds do in fact 'relate to' the world in any way at all, let alone in such a way as to give us the possibility of gaining knowledge of it.

(ii) Detachment and insulation

Despite his own aims, Locke's views seem to commit him to a detachment picture that is even more radical than the insulation picture to which Descartes commits himself.

Descartes regards his thoughts and experiences as of such a kind that he could have had them *whether or not* the world exists and *however* the world exists. As we saw, this means that his views threaten to 'insulate' the mind from the world, to shield the one from exposure to the other, to protect the mind from being affected by the ways the world is, so that the one is incapable of relating to the other.

Locke however regards the mind as of such a kind that it is incapable of reaching beyond its own contents, beyond 'ideas' with their distinct and peculiar characteristics. So his conception is more radical: unlike Descartes, he threatens to 'detach' the mind from the world altogether, wholly to cut off the one from the other.

(iii) Knowledge and language

Locke's position imposes heavy restrictions on what we know and can know. Again, it is easiest to appreciate this by contrast with Descartes. According to Descartes, we can know things without appeal to experience; indeed, he urges us to construct the foundations of knowledge without appeal to experience. Locke's empiricism obliges him to resist here: there is no knowledge without appeal to experience. But Locke's position on the nature and limits of thought threatens to go much further: to insist that we cannot use whatever experience we do have to think beyond – let alone gain knowledge of what is beyond – our own minds.

The issues ramify when we consider language, communication and the transmission of thoughts. For Locke takes the view that meaningful words stand for ideas in the mind of the one using them. If this is correct, and communication between two people is possible, then the ideas for which words stand must be shareable. Otherwise there is no possibility of meeting a basic requirement for communication: that one person knows what another means. But Locke conceives of ideas as logically private contents of the mind and hence not shareable. Moreover, he insists that we cannot think beyond the simple ideas of sensation and reflection. So his views threaten to undermine the very possibility of communication.

One consequence is that it becomes difficult to see how he could possibly achieve his basic aim, of clearing a way for the progress of science. For there seems to be no way of achieving even the most basic requirement for this: that he communicate his views to others so that others know what he means.

Just as Descartes undermines his own remedy for the sceptical situation in the Trojan Horse way by drawing insulation into the heart of his position, so Locke undermines his own attempt to shrug off that situation by drawing detachment into the heart of his position. By precluding the possibility of our being related to the world in the ways required for our thoughts to be about the world beyond us, he plunges us fully into the sceptical situation without any possibility of escape.

5. Possible paths to pursue

Locke's *Essay* contains a number of sections that shed light on the passages discussed in this chapter. See in particular the discussion of 'ideas' (Book II, Chapter 1, §§1–5) and perception (II, 9, §§1–5), Locke's revealing (or misleading?) fancy about the 'dark room' of the understanding (II, 11, §17) and his account of 'the signification of words' (III, 2, §§1–5), of the extent of our knowledge (IV, 3, §§1–5) and its reality (IV, 4, §§1–3) and of the knowledge we may acquire about the 'existence of other things' (IV, 11, §1–2).

The best guide to Locke is Michael Ayers' *Locke: Epistemology and Ontology*, first published as two volumes but now available as one. It is a long and intense study, but it is possible to dip in and out, treating the chapters as essays that stand on their own. A more immediately accessible guide is E. J. Lowe *Locke on Human Understanding*, but be aware that the interpretation of Locke on ideas and perception is controversial (it is perhaps what Locke ought to have said, but it is not evidently what he does say). An excellent collection of papers about all aspects of Locke is Vere Chappell's (ed.) *Locke*. Jonathan Dancy pursues the issues concerning empiricism and perception to the present day in his *Introduction to Contemporary Epistemology* (chapters 6 and 11).

Radical III

Action

4

How we live and work

Karl Marx (1818–83) worked on his *Economic and Philosophical Manuscripts* in 1844 in Paris, hence their nicknames: the *Paris Manuscripts* or the *1844 Manuscripts*. They were unknown until first published by the Soviet editor David Ryazanov in 1932, when they substantially altered received views about Marx. They reflect a period of considerable upheaval in Marx's life and fertility in his thought. There is still an air of excitement and mystery about them.

The manuscripts consist of about 50,000 words of draft material on a variety of topics, including labour, private property, communism and money. Together, they form a first version of Marx's lifelong project, the critique of political economy. In contrast with his later work, the manuscripts offer rich and resonant descriptions of what it feels like to live and work under capitalism, and that is why we shall look into them. But they do raise difficulties, being fragmentary, somewhat disorganized and deploying old philosophical terms for new purposes. We shall have to go slowly, first identifying the key elements and then attending closely to Marx's arguments.

The manuscripts are very evidently the work of a philosophical radical, combining all the essential elements. There is great audacity here, an urge to get to the root of things, and a determination to be thoroughly engaged with fundamental issues that matter to us all. But Marx's way of doing radical philosophy is very different from that of Descartes or Locke. The pressing issues in the passages we shall examine are fully practical. The point of entering into philosophy is to change our living conditions, not to clear the way for science or find foundational principles of knowledge. Marx takes his stand not on reasoned reflection or experience but on action.

1. Alienation

We need to understand our living conditions under capitalism, to see clearly what they are and to discover what causes them and keeps them in place.

(i) Labour

Marx launches his inquiry with a particular question:

> What does the externalization of labour consist of? (137; all page references in this chapter are to Karl Marx's *Economic and Philosophical Manuscripts of 1844*; see the Bibliography for full details)

To understand his argument, which is an answer to this question, we need first to understand exactly what it is he is asking. By 'labour', he means more specifically labour under the conditions of capitalism. And by 'externalization', he means the way that human beings naturally project themselves into nature through their productive activity.

There is a whole variety of ways we so project ourselves, of course. Our modes of productive activity can be presented on a spectrum. Some modes are essentially positive. They offer us the opportunity to realize ourselves, by giving us scope to use and develop our talents, to exercise our abilities and to acquire new ones. Indeed, at one end of the spectrum, our free productive activity gives us the chance to become fully aware of ourselves and to contemplate a world that is partly of our own making. A person may use their sculptor's ability to create a statue, for example, and thus learn something about themselves and what they are capable of, while also fashioning something new in the world, something that enriches it for them.

At the other end of the spectrum, some modes of productive activity are essentially negative. They deny us the opportunity to realize ourselves, by restricting the exercise of our abilities and by preventing us from acquiring new ones. Indeed, our forced productive activity can distort our relations so deeply that we come to think not only of the world but also of our own selves as hostile and alien to ourselves. A person on an assembly-line, for example, may be forced to repeat exactly the same simple move on the same semi-formed and ugly object countless times every hour, thus acquiring and developing no real skill and rendering themselves too exhausted and unimaginative to acquire new abilities, learning nothing about themselves and doing nothing that enriches the world, so that they come to hate their life, their activity, their world and finally themselves. This is what we shall mean by 'alienation', not just any form of externalization but a condition of deep estrangement, in which, through their own labour, people are divided from themselves and from others, their world, their own activity and its products.

Towards the middle of the spectrum are modes of externalization – of projecting oneself onto the world – that may be neutral. Selling something would be like this if it neither offered nor denied us much opportunity to realize ourselves. For example, a person might sell an inherited statue in a society where the structures and relations that permit commerce are not themselves alienating.

What sort of productive activity is work under capitalism? Where on our spectrum is it located? That is the question Marx is raising.

(ii) Under capitalism, work alienates one from one's own produce, world and activity

Marx's claim is that work under capitalism places one in the condition of alienation, deep estrangement. Through their own labour, people are divided from themselves and from others, their world, their own activity and its products.

Marx offers an extended set of observations about this. Together, they depict the alienation condition as a series of concentric circles, with the self as its inner focus:

What does the externalization of labour consist of then?

Firstly, that labour is exterior to the worker, that is, it does not belong to his essence. Therefore he does not confirm himself in his work, he denies himself, feels miserable instead of happy, deploys no

free physical and intellectual energy, but mortifies his body and ruins
his mind. (137)

In describing the outer rings, Marx concentrates his analysis on the
elements of compulsion, drawing attention to the ways that external
powers impinge on one, forcing one to work and to live in certain
ways. So he describes the kind of alienation that comes from finding no
source of satisfaction in what one produces, no confirmation of one's
value in having produced things.

Marx also analyses the alienation that comes from feeling one's own
world is hostile to one, that it is an environment composed of demands
on one's time and energy that come from outside oneself and with
which one cannot identify:

> Thus the worker only feels at home outside his work and in his work
> he feels a stranger. He is at home when he is not working and when
> he works he is not at home. His labour is therefore not voluntary but
> compulsory, forced labour. (137)

Closely surrounding the self at the centre of these concentric rings
of alienation is the sense that comes from feeling one's actions are
forced on one, not what one would have chosen, perhaps even forced
out of one. This too is characteristic of work under capitalism: in such
circumstances, one's activity does not express one's autonomy and one's
actions may not feel like one's *own* actions.

(iii) In these conditions, work alienates one from one's own self

Marx then strengthens his position. Work under capitalism places one
also in the inner rings of the alienation condition:

> [Labour] is therefore not the satisfaction of a need but only a means to
> satisfy needs outside itself. How alien it really is, is very evident from
> the fact that when there is no physical or other compulsion, labour
> is avoided like the plague. External labour, labour in which man

externalizes himself, is a labour of self-sacrifice and mortification. (137)

Here he concentrates his analysis on the elements of inner inertia, drawing attention to the ways that one may be deprived of the ability or opportunity to resist the external powers that impinge on one, thus allowing those outer elements free play. So he describes the kind of alienation that comes from the fact that one's work does not satisfy any need of *one's own* (or at least, it does not appear that the need being satisfied is one's own).

At the centre of the rings of alienation, more intimate than the sense that one's *actions* do not belong to oneself, and hence are not one's own, is the feeling that one's *self* does not belong to oneself, and hence is not one's own:

> Finally, the external character of labour for the worker shows itself in the fact that it is not his own but someone else's, that it does not belong to him, that he does not belong to himself in his labour but to someone else. (137)

There are weaker and stronger conditions of this innermost alienation. In the weaker, given that one does not belong to oneself, there is a sense that one is divided *from* oneself, in some complex way *alien* to oneself, a stranger. In the stronger, there is a sense that one is divided *against* oneself, in some complex way *hostile* to oneself, an enemy. Marx thinks it characteristic of work under capitalism that it places one in both conditions of innermost alienation:

> As in religion the human imagination's own activity, the activity of man's head and his heart, reacts independently on the individual as an alien activity of gods or devils, so the activity of the worker is not his own spontaneous activity. It belongs to another and is the loss of himself. (137)

(iv) To be alienated in these ways is to be deprived of a genuinely human existence

> The result we arrive at then is that man (the worker) only feels himself freely active in his animal functions of eating, drinking, and

procreating, at most also in his dwelling and dress, and feels himself an animal in his human functions. (137–8)

One way that Marx measures the harm of the alienation condition is by pointing out the way it deprives us of a genuinely human existence. He does this by appeal to the absolute divide that he draws between human existence and animal existence (or *mere* animal existence as we might say, for clarity's sake).

We share with other animals the basic needs to eat, drink and procreate. In a genuinely human existence, these functions make us feel human and precisely *not* animal. This is because, in a genuinely human existence, we do not engage in these acts merely to satisfy these basic needs. Eating, drinking and procreating take place in a larger context formed by a complex of activities in which we are free to engage. This freedom enables us to perform these acts for fun, for intimacy, for the creation and sustaining of social bonds and so on. Marx's claim is that one of the freedoms that the alienation condition strips us of is the freedom to engage in this larger context.

Eating, drinking, procreating, etc. are indeed truly human functions. But in the abstraction that separates them from the other round of human activity and makes them into final and exclusive ends they become animal. (138)

In the alienation condition, these functions can only be 'basic needs'. Performing them just becomes the satisfying of these needs. And this makes us feel precisely *not* human but animal.

This combines the two strands of Marx's thought. On the one hand, there are his arguments from the character of work under capitalism: that one is placed in several concentric rings of alienation that together make up the alienation condition. On the other hand, there is his argument from the human/mere animal distinction: that living in the alienation condition deprives one of a genuinely human existence. Together, they lead him to conclude that work under capitalism deprives one of a genuinely human existence.

(v) **Summary**

Marx argues that people enter into a drastic form of alienation, one in which they are divided from others, their world, their own activity and its products, and even themselves, so that nothing that they do or relate with has meaning for them, and even what they are has little or no significance or value. In this 'alienation condition', people lose their humanity and become (merely) animal. And Marx's point in putting it like this is to communicate a sense of urgency: the alienation condition is one that must be overcome. He thinks the condition calls for careful analysis, by philosophy and other disciplines, as well as strenuous measures. We have to understand exactly what brings the alienation condition about, and (what will become of steadily greater significance) how it is kept in place.

Marx's alienation condition is a dramatic possibility within the context of the practical, just as Descartes' sceptical situation is a dramatic possibility within the context of the theoretical. But it is worth noting that, in one respect at least, the alienation condition is worse than the sceptical situation. In the depths of the sceptical situation, as Descartes conceives it, there is still a single united self, capable of engaging in a single and united way in the activity of doubting and of then reflecting on the implications of that doubting. In the depths of the alienation condition, on the other hand, the self is divided against itself and thus quite incapable of engaging in a single and united way in any activity, let alone in reflection on implications.

2. Wider context

Some questions inevitably arise when we consider this argument. What *is* a genuinely human existence? What are the socio-economic and political conditions that would make it possible? Marx's critique of capitalism fits into a broader, more positive project because it includes an attempt to address these questions.

For Marx, a genuinely human existence is one in which we lead actively self-realizing lives. To understand what he has in mind, it is helpful to distinguish – however crudely – between (i) natural abilities we are born with (such as the ability to perceive the world using our five senses) and (ii) natural abilities we have to acquire (such as learning to use language). Abilities of both sorts exist in relation to opportunities; if we are to exercise (or, in the latter case, acquire) abilities, we need opportunities to do so. But abilities of the first sort are wholly un-free: given the opportunity to exercise them, they *must* be exercised. Whereas abilities of the second sort offer two kinds of freedom: given the opportunity, one can *choose* to exercise them; and having acquired some, one can acquire more. This is not to deny that there are some elements of constraint with most acquired abilities; for example, they usually involve conditioning or some form of education which is not, and perhaps could not be, freely chosen by the individuals themselves.

In active self-realization, one has the opportunity to acquire powers and abilities fully and freely, to exercise them and to be able to make them evident to others. Quite how extensive this set of powers and abilities has to be for the individual to count as self-realized is controversial. It will partly depend on the individual concerned.

We will return to these issues. For our immediate purposes, it is enough to appreciate that – in Marx's view – what is wrong with the alienation condition is that it obstructs active self-realization, or blocks it altogether. That is why living in this condition deprives one of a genuinely human existence. That is what is wrong with an economic system that places one in this condition.

(i) Exploitation, alienation and identity

Not every bad economic system places one in the alienation condition, in which one is divided from others, one's world, one's own activity and its products, and even oneself. A system can be deeply exploitative, for example, without being alienating. To appreciate Marx's critique of capitalism, and to understand the alienation condition more closely, it helps to see why.

Marx thinks that work under capitalism is in almost every respect an improvement over work under feudalism. But the particular features that cause capitalism to deprive people of a genuinely human existence were not present in the economic system that preceded it. Though undoubtedly deeply exploitative, feudalism is not alienating. The explanation lies with the role played by identity.

Setting aside complicating features, the basic situation in feudalism is one in which a person, A, is subject to another person, B. A is a serf, say, and B is his lord. This system operates in virtue of *who people are* (and were born to be, at least as all concerned believed) and is not mediated; A is directly subject to B. This form of subjection is dependent on, and a constant reminder of, certain simple and fixed identities: who is a serf, and what kind of life this entails; who is a lord, and what kind of life this entails. Now these settled identities badly distort the way in which human beings ought to live together. But in so far as serfs and lords believe they are born to these roles in life, and are committed to finding value in living out these roles, fulfilling what is required of each, the particular kinds of alienation associated with capitalism do not afflict them. What they do or produce is a reminder of their identity (no matter how wretched that identity is), and hence it can be a source of satisfaction and confirmation, making them at home in their world (no matter how wretched that world is), so that they are not divided against others or themselves. Because their actions contain this constant reminder and confirmation of their identity, Marx thought, they do not live in the alienation condition. In short, where subjection exploits identity, being dependent on precisely who one is, exploitation can occur without alienation.

The same conditions do not obtain in the more developed economic system of capitalism. In particular, subjection does not exploit identity in this direct way that reminds and confirms one in *who one is*. Setting aside complicating features again, the basic situation in capitalism remains one in which a person, A, is subject to another person, B. But

A is made subject to B via some other thing, x, rather than directly or in virtue of who A is or who B is. For example, A might be a car mechanic, subject to the garage-owner B in virtue of the fact that B owns the machines and the tools without which A could not operate as a car mechanic. The value of x might be any of a vast range of non-human assets, so long as they can be owned and exchanged in some market: machinery, infrastructure, patents, agricultural land, residential real estate, commercial inventory, mutual funds, bonds, stocks, insurance policies, pension funds and so on – that is, 'capital'. This is a mediated form of subjection that displaces identity; it occurs in virtue of *what x is* (in virtue of the ownership of capital) rather than who the people involved are. And since it displaces identity, Marx thought, such work is predisposed to being alienating: not to confirm who one is or to form a world in which the person one takes oneself to be is at home, but instead to divide one from others and from oneself. In short, where subjection does not exploit identity, being independent of precisely who one is, exploitation can occur with – may even adopt the form of – alienation.

(ii) Alienation

Marx describes the alienation condition as one in which we are divided from others, our world, our own activity and its products, and even ourselves. These are the claims we shall concentrate on. But Marx's full analysis of the condition extends beyond this, and it is worth getting an impression of how the features we are now aware of fit into a larger pattern.

In the alienation condition, we are divided from *(a) the products of our labour* – they are alien to us in that they exercise power over us; *(b) the world* – where this includes both the raw material for transformation into products and the collectivity of products: both are alien to us in that they are opposed and hostile to us; *(c) our own activity* – it is alien to us in that it is independent of us, does not belong to us and is directed against us (a 'procreation that is castration'); *(d) our own desires* – they are alien to us in that we do not choose them; they are imposed on us; we want things we do not necessarily want to want; we do not identify with or endorse our desires; our desires seem to master us; our desires seem confused, puzzling, mysterious; our desires seem to lead us to unhappiness, dissatisfaction; *(e) our own selves* – as the life and essence that both make us the individuals we are and make us members of the human species – it is alien to us in that it is only a means to the satisfaction of a need, our existence (and merely our *physical* existence); *(f) our own bodies* – they are alien to us in that they are part of nature, of the world, of that which is already alien to us; *(g) other human beings* – they are alien to us in that they are opposed to us, just as we are opposed to ourselves.

(iii) 'Mere' animals

Human beings are, as such, a species. Now we can characterize this species in various ways – for example by its biological, and eventually genetic, features. But Marx seems to have a more general consideration in mind, characterizing species by the kinds of activity they engage in. It is worth clarifying this aspect of his proposals, expanding on them in ways that are consistent with what he says.

In his view, what distinguishes the kinds of activity human beings engage in – and hence what characterizes them as a species – is their freedom (we do not always *have* to do what we *can* do – we can sometimes choose not to exercise the powers and abilities we have) and conscious reflectiveness (we do not *just* eat, sleep, procreate, etc., nor are we just consciously aware of doing so, but we are able to reflect on what it is to do so, why we do it, etc.).

As a consequence, we human beings are born with the possibility of having a significant *distance* from biological necessities, the kinds of thing imposed on any animal (e.g. the need to eat, sleep, procreate). For while all animals have to do these things at some level, we human beings can still *reflect* on doing what we do, on being the animals we are; we can to some extent *choose* what we do, how we do it, when and so on. Indeed, we can ask *why* we have to do it, how best to go about doing it and so on. And in these and other ways, it makes sense to describe us as having lives to lead, whereas most other animals are led *by* their lives.

Now this distance from biological necessities is what we, as human beings, are born to. We start with those special natural abilities which enable us to acquire other abilities, such as language use and reasoning, on which our freedom and conscious reflectiveness – and hence our distance from biological necessities – depend. But this distance – this freedom and conscious reflectiveness – is something we can be deprived of altogether; or it is at least something we can be deprived of the *sense* of having. And this is what, according to Marx, occurs with alienation. Either we are forced to live in such a way that we are *not* free or reflective, or we are forced to live *as if* we were not free or reflective (e.g. to forget or ignore the fact that we are). And this occurs in the usual ways with which we are now familiar – by being exploited in such a way that we lose autonomy over what we do and what we desire.

3. Questions

Marx's sketch of the effects of work under capitalism moves fast and assumes much. Whether conditions were as bad or as general as he describes in the mid-nineteenth century and whether they continue to be at the start of the twenty-first are controversial issues. Part of Marx's intention in describing the alienation condition is to create a sense of urgency, to recognize the necessity of radical change, but what he writes ought first to induce a sense of caution and the need for reflection. Is there too much reliance on limited evidence, leading to unwarranted generalization? Is there a background of unrealistic utopianism? Is there a tendency to exaggeration that undermines the analysis itself? To recognize such issues is not necessarily to take up a wholly negative stance. We may be attracted by the general features of Marx's position and still appreciate that his analysis must present the conditions of work under capitalism accurately if the remedy he then describes is to count as such.

(i) Work under capitalism is alienating?

This is not the place to pursue the historical investigations necessary to substantiate or dismiss Marx's claims. What we can do is point out how very extreme the evidence of facts about the world might have to be to bear out his analysis.

Our previous comments give us scope for at least three strategies to accommodate even the most hostile descriptions of work under capitalism while denying that such work is *both* generally and deeply alienating, as Marx claims it is. Such strategies can be used against Marx's own descriptions of mid-nineteenth-century Europe, or subsequent descriptions covering any other time or place up to the present. Not all are equally plausible, of course, and we shall find reason to question various aspects of each, but it is helpful to have an idea of the different ways that Marx's analysis might be vulnerable.

The three strategies share to varying degrees a basic thought. If we are considering people in general, then there are many for whom work under capitalism is not alienating at all. And if we are considering the alienated, and particularly the deeply alienated, the problem is a particular one, limited, circumscribed, absolutely non-general.

(a) Externalizing, but not in a bad way

We might claim that, at any given time or place, there are many whose productive activity – taken as a whole – is essentially positive. Many of those who work long hours but have families and children might say this. Theirs may not be the world-enriching work of a sculptor, but who could insist that it should be? Their work is satisfying enough, develops talents, exercises abilities and enables them to contemplate a world partly of their own making. In short, this strategy claims that the *externalization of labour characteristic of capitalism* is not both generally and deeply alienating.

(b) Exploitative, but not in a bad way

We might borrow from an argument that may resemble Hegel. Not that one need insist that people *must* be exploited to be unified with their activities and self. A modified form of the argument would be sufficient to accommodate even the most hostile descriptions of work under capitalism. We might claim that being exploited is not – or at least *need not be* – inconsistent with being unified with one's activities and self. Many are unified despite (and perhaps even because of) being exploited. In short, this strategy claims that the *exploitation characteristic of capitalism* is not both generally and deeply alienating.

(c) Mediated, but not in a bad way

We might point out that capitalism is capable of equipping itself with similar features to those that made feudalism palatable to the exploited majority. It may be true that capitalism is in effect a mediated form of subjection, but it does not follow that this is the way that the subjected explain their state, let alone how they think or feel about it. For capitalism can and does exploit identity no less than feudalism; it merely does so in more complex and fluid ways. An employee A might be subject to employee B in virtue of their role in some firm, for example. This role comes with a status, title and set of entitlements by which they identify themselves, so that this system too may be said to operate in virtue of who people are – at least as far as what really matters is concerned: the way that the employees explain themselves to themselves and others; how they think and feel about themselves. What they then do or produce can act as a reminder of that identity, and hence count as a source of satisfaction and confirmation, something that can make them feel at home in their world and not divided against others or themselves. In short, this strategy claims that *the mediation characteristic of capitalism* is not both generally and deeply alienating.

(ii) Marx's argument from avoidance

This is Marx's one clear argument for the claim that work under capitalism is alienating:

> How alien it really is, is very evident from the fact that when there is no physical or other compulsion, labour is avoided like the plague. (137–8)

But this is a dangerous argument for Marx to deploy. For there are many activities that people 'avoid like the plague' when not coerced by some means or other, not just exploitative work. For example, a good deal of our basic education usually takes this form, without which we could not become and continue to be actively self-realizing. This is apparently a common human characteristic, found in all previous economic systems, so it seems very unlikely that it would change whenever capitalism gives way to another economic system. So Marx must either allow that avoidance is *not* a sufficient guide to what is alienating (and thus give up his one clear argument for the claim that work under capitalism is alienating) or accept that active self-realization itself is alienating (and thus give up his one clear argument for the claim that capitalism must and will give way to another economic system).

(iii) Alienation deprives one of a genuinely human existence?

Marx's appeal to eating, drinking and procreating as a way of measuring the harm done by the alienation condition is more complex than it may at first appear. It may even undermine itself. For suppose we accept that, under capitalism, some worker's human activities really do become those of a mere animal. Evidently, 'mere' animals are not alienated. So should we not conclude that this worker is *not* alienated?

Or we could apply pressure from a different direction. Evidently, 'mere' animals are not alienated when they engage in these acts merely to satisfy their basic needs. So what is alienating for human beings when they do so? Presumably the fact that they are aware that this ought not to be the case, that as human beings their eating, drinking and procreating ought to take place in a larger context of activities in which we are free to engage. But then they only feel alienated to the extent that they are still capable of recognizing that they are human and not animal. So it seems that Marx must either allow that alienated human beings do not become animal in their eating, drinking and procreating, or accept that those human beings who do succeed in becoming animal in their eating, drinking and procreating are not alienated. Either way, we may question this argument for the claim that alienation deprives one of a genuinely human existence.

4. Wider concerns

(i) Descriptive and normative

Marx's main conclusion, that work in conditions of capitalism deprives one of a genuinely human existence, is susceptible to interpretation, and thus to varying forms of challenge. Two versions are particularly worth examining.

On the first ('descriptive') version, what Marx is saying is that we are deprived of a genuinely human existence because we *are actually and in fact* alienated from our own products and activities and world and selves, because of the particular conditions of exploitation under which we are obliged to work. And the main challenge to his view, on this interpretation of it, lies in pointing out that very many of the people supposedly so affected do not actually and in fact *regard* themselves as deprived in this way, nor alienated, nor even exploited. Not that there need be any contradiction in claiming both that A is exploited and that A does not regard himself as exploited (just as A can be red in the face without realizing he is). But there does seem to be something strange about the idea both that A is alienated and that A does not regard himself as alienated. There seems to be an internal relation between being in an alienation condition and feeling alienated, just as there is between being in a pained condition and feeling pained. The issue is not clear-cut, but as a first pass, there does seem to be something intuitive about this thought; that it would be as nonsensical to say 'I may be alienated, but I don't feel I am' as it would be to say 'I may be in pain, but I don't feel I am'.

On the alternative ('normative') version, what Marx is really getting at is that we *ought* to feel alienated from our own products and activities and world and selves, given the particular conditions of exploitation under which we are obliged to work. This answers the main challenge to the descriptive view, tacitly accepting that there is an internal relation between being alienated and feeling alienated. But it opens up a large gap between the premises and the conclusion of Marx's argument. For once we accept that very many people do not *feel* alienated, and hence (on this version) *are* not alienated, we have no reason to conclude that we are, actually and in fact, deprived of a genuinely human existence. It may make a difference to accept that everyone *ought to* feel alienated, but not the kind of difference that would save *this* conclusion.

(ii) Alienation and contradiction

What makes the alienation condition so much worse than the sceptical situation is that the self is divided against itself. So even when the simplest patterns of thought are attempted, they cannot be ascribed to the same single self. This has worrying consequences for Marx that we can spell out by considering what is required for argument.

In order to draw the conclusion of any argument (our own or someone else's) from its premises, one must be capable of ascribing thoughts to oneself, the same single thing that endures at least as long as the thought pattern lasts. Suppose I am not capable of this – suppose I am in the alienation condition, for example. Then I will not even be able to think an argument of so simple a form as 'I think that p (e.g. that I am doubting); if I think that p, I ought to think that q (e.g. I exist); therefore I ought to think that q'. For there is no single thing to which these uses of 'I' refer. So the closest I could get would be an argument of the form 'a thinks that p; if b thinks that p, he ought to think that q; so c ought to think that q'. And arguments of this form are obviously fallacious (more specifically enthymematic, since they need an extra premise – unavailable in the alienation condition – 'a = b = c'); there are any number of possible situations in which all the premises are true and yet the conclusion is false.

The worrying consequence is then obvious. Suppose we draw the conclusion of Marx's argument from his premises: that we are in the alienation condition. Then what we have supposed cannot be true. If it were true (that we are in the alienation condition), then it must be false (that we are in the alienation condition). For anyone capable of drawing the conclusion of an argument from its premises cannot be in the alienation condition, in which the self is divided against itself.

5. Possible paths to pursue

This chapter has focused on the 1844 Paris manuscripts and hence avoided appeal to the later Marx, but readers interested in his development will keep both in mind. For context, read the edited version of the 1844 manuscripts in *Karl Marx: Selected Writings* (McLellan ed.) together with selections from other works of the same pre-1848 period collected there, particularly *The German Ideology* and *The Poverty of Philosophy*. In the later Marx, the following parts of *Capital* (Volume 1) are particularly relevant to themes covered here: chapter 10 (on the working day), chapter 14 (on the capitalist character of manufacture), chapter 15 (on the tension between worker and machine) and chapter 32 (on the tendencies of capitalist accumulation).

An outstanding guide to Marx is *Karl Marx's Theory of History: A Defence* by G. A. Cohen. Its combination of analytical clarity and attack makes it a joy to work through. Though focusing on the later work, it has much to say about alienation and related issues. An old and classic guide to the history of political theory that sets Marx in his context is the three-volume *Man and Society* by John Plamenatz (Marx appears in the third volume, chapters 3–5). Due to the fragmentary nature of the Paris manuscripts, it is particularly necessary to consult good biographies: *Karl Marx: His Life and Thought* by David McLellan is a thorough life-and-work, but it might best be approached now by the more thoroughly readable *Karl Marx* by Francis Wheen or the more recent *A World to Win: The Life and Works of Karl Marx* by Sven-Eric

Liedman. For a very critical perspective on the alienation material, see Jon Elster's *Making Sense of Marx* (Part I) and *An Introduction to Karl Marx* (chapter 3). The Hegel argument mentioned above, which turns on the analogy with Lordship and Bondage in Hegel's *Phenomenology of Spirit* has been much discussed, and the most disparate interpretations abound. One of the clearest and most accessible accounts is also one of the most plausible, as an interpretation of Hegel: Peter Singer's *Hegel* (chapter 4).

5

How we might live and work

Karl Marx's thought developed considerably during and after his work on the 1844 Paris manuscripts. The period can seem to mark a brutal divide between his earlier and later career, but it is perhaps better seen as an unusually intense phase within an essentially continuous development.

One aspect of continuity here is Marx's early fascination with false consciousness, which would grow later into a more systematic theory of 'ideology' (Marx was the first to use the term for the purpose). The notion is still rather narrow and under-specified in February 1844, when Marx described religion as false consciousness. But the Paris manuscripts contain glimpses of the core notion: the general phenomenon by which we become complicit with forces that conceal our alienation from us, thus lessening the frustration we ought rationally to feel at the way the world is arranged. This is one theme we shall take up in the present chapter.

Another theme we shall take up also links the earlier and later work. By the time of the Paris manuscripts, Marx's turn from a positive to a negative view of philosophy is clearly well underway. Far from being a means towards liberation, philosophy is already being identified as part of those conditions of alienation from which we need to be liberated.

The most important aspect of continuity, and the main focus of this chapter, is Marx's early concern to go beyond what it feels like to live and work under capitalism. The Paris manuscripts contain visionary moments where he presents communism both as a prediction of the way the world is developing and as a remedy for the present condition of the world. Again, the account becomes clearer and more forceful by 1848 with *The Communist Manifesto*. But the manuscripts contain clear evidence that, from early on, Marx has much the same optimism and audacity as Descartes: the remedy for a bad situation lies not in flight from it but in total immersion within it.

The idea is that work under capitalism places us in the alienation condition, but this condition can be made to undermine itself. For immersion in what divides people from themselves and others leads to revolution and – in its most developed form – a communism that will unite people:

> communism as the positive abolition of private property and thus of human self-alienation and therefore the real reappropriation of the human essence by and for man. (148; all page references in this chapter are to Karl Marx's *Economic and Philosophical Manuscripts of 1844*; see the Bibliography for full details)

Communism in this form is the remedy for work under capitalism because it reverses each of the divisive effects of the alienation condition. It unites us with others, our world, our own activity and its products, and ourselves. Thus communism in this form makes it possible for what we do to have meaning for us, for what we are to have significance and value for us.

1. Communism

(i) Descriptive and normative

When he addresses capitalism and its remedy, Marx offers two very different kinds of argument. To appreciate his position, we need first to understand the distinction between these kinds and then the possibility of their combination in a single theory.

Marx's first kind of argument aims at telling us why capitalism *will* be overthrown and communism instituted in its place. One example is

Marx's general theory of modes of production, which claims to show that capitalism is inefficient. Another example is Marx's theory of class struggle, which claims to show that capitalism is exploitative. We can think of this kind of argument as 'descriptive', since it sets out to describe as accurately as possible what is or will be the case. Deciding whether or not arguments of this kind succeed depends on obtaining and correctly interpreting facts about the world (empirical data). So we appeal to the social sciences more than to philosophy to judge the strength of these kinds of argument.

Marx's second kind of argument falls squarely within the scope of philosophy. This kind aims at telling us why capitalism *should* be overthrown and communism instituted in its place. We have already examined one example: in his theory of alienation, Marx claims that capitalism deprives us of a genuinely human existence and thus should be overthrown. Notice that this kind of argument is totally different from one that aims to give an accurate account of the facts about the world. It does not set out to *describe* what is or will be the case but to *propose* what should be the case. The label for this kind of argument is 'normative'.

Descriptive arguments set out to describe what is or will be the case, and history may prove them wrong. Indeed, according to some, history has already shown that Marx's descriptive arguments fail. Whether this is how we are to interpret the collapse of the former USSR is controversial, of course. What Marx actually predicted in *A Contribution to the Critique of Political Economy* is that a capitalist society will not give way to a genuinely communist one unless and until capitalism is fully developed in that society and the higher relations which characterize socialism have matured within that society. Now neither of these features had been achieved in Russia at the time of the 1917 revolution. So it might be said that the failure of the former USSR is less a counter-instance to Marx's descriptive arguments than a partial confirmation of them.

Normative arguments, by contrast, are not vulnerable in the same way to history. They do not set out to describe what is or will be the case, so facts about the way the world is or will be need not undermine them. No amount of facts about how capitalism *has* survived will be sufficient to show that it *should* survive. The most such facts could show is that capitalism *will* survive. Equally, no amount of argument showing why capitalism *should* be overthrown is sufficient to show that it *will* be overthrown.

Nevertheless, there is room for complexity. It is perfectly possible for the reasons that a normative argument gives as to why capitalism *should* be overthrown to turn out to be the very same reasons that a descriptive argument gives as to why capitalism *will* be overthrown. Such a theory would have a dual aspect, being possessed of both normative and descriptive arguments.

(ii) Communism is the solution to the alienation condition

Marx's theory of alienation, fully understood, is just such a dual-aspect theory. Capitalism places us in the alienation condition, thus depriving us of a genuinely human existence. And this reason why capitalism *should* be overthrown is also the very reason why capitalism *will* be overthrown. For immersion in alienation and what divides us will lead to what unites us: first in frustration and anger and destructive activity (with the aim of bringing capitalism down) and then in hope and fervour and productive activity (with the aim of bringing communism forth). This is why Marx describes communism, in its developed form, as *positive*: 'the positive abolition of private property and thus of human self-alienation and therefore the real reappropriation of the human essence by and for man'.

> This is communism as the complete and conscious return of man conserving all the riches of previous development for man himself as a social, that is human being. (148)

In the alienation condition, we are divided from others, our world, our own activity and its products, and even ourselves, with the result that we are deprived of a genuinely human existence and lose our true nature.

> Communism as completed naturalism is humanism and as completed
> humanism is naturalism. It is the genuine solution of the antagonism
> between man and nature and between man and man. (148)

Communism can present itself as the solution, the remedy, because it
returns us to human existence (*completed humanism*) and thus to our true
nature (*completed naturalism*). In instituting an economic system based
on the abolition of private property, communism will unite us with others,
with our world, with our own activity and its products, and with ourselves.
And this in turn makes it possible for what we do and relate with to have
meaning for us, and what we are to have significance and value.

This dual-aspect nature of his theory of alienation, as fully
understood, gives Marx reason to be strikingly optimistic, audacious.
If it is true that the reason why capitalism *will* be overthrown (that
it deprives us of a genuinely human existence) is the reason why it
should be overthrown, then the remedy can be immersion in the
alienation condition rather than in flight from it. Or as Marx puts it in
the conclusion to *The Communist Manifesto*: what capitalists actually
produce are their own gravediggers.

Thus there is a striking similarity between Marx confronting the
alienation condition and Descartes facing the sceptical situation. Both
are convinced that a bad situation will undermine itself, that the route
to a remedy lies through the awfulness rather than skirting around it.

(iii) Communism is humanism and naturalism

Marx's claim that 'Communism as completed naturalism is humanism
and as completed humanism is naturalism' needs unpacking. The idea
is that, for us to live a genuinely *human* existence just is for us to live the
life that is *proper* to us as human beings, and hence the life that it is our
nature to live. So, in enabling us to live the one kind of life, communism
enables us to live the other kind also.

In overthrowing the alienation condition, for example, communism
enables us to live a genuinely human existence, and thus counts as
'completed humanism'. And since to enable us to live such an existence

just is to enable us to live the life that is proper to us as human beings, the life that it is our nature to live, communism counts as 'completed naturalism'.

We get some insight into what Marx means by a genuinely human existence in two ways: by recalling that his model of an alienated life for human beings is the life of a 'mere' animal, and by noting two additional comments he makes here:

> I can in practice only relate myself humanly to an object if the object relates itself humanly to man. (152)

And

> Man does not lose himself in his object provided that it is a human object or objective humanity. This is only possible if it becomes a social object for him and he himself becomes a social being, while society becomes a being for him in this object. (152)

Putting these claims together, the idea seems to be this. A 'mere' animal engages in eating, drinking and procreating to satisfy these basic needs. Human beings, on the other hand, can perform these acts for recreation, amusement, intimacy and so on. In so doing, they relate humanly to other human beings and other human beings relate humanly to them. Human beings are not able to exercise these abilities in any and all circumstances. They require opportunities that only the right kind of social relations can offer. Where such relations exist, it is possible for human beings to engage freely in acts that more than satisfy their basic needs. In the alienation condition, such relations do not exist, and indeed they could not exist, for the conditions for their possibility are withdrawn. In communism, such relations do exist. Indeed, it is on the possibility of such relations that communism – as completed humanism and completed naturalism – both depends and thrives.

But these comments also raise problems. The claim that objects must relate themselves humanly to me for me to relate myself humanly to them will turn out to be a root problem with Marx's position.

(iv) Philosophy could not solve the alienation condition

Philosophizing comes off rather poorly in Marx's account. This is not surprising, perhaps, given the nature of capitalism and the alienation condition it brings about:

> It can be seen how the solution of theoretical opposition is only possible in a practical way, only through the practical energy of man. (153)

Capitalism and the alienation condition are not susceptible to the kinds of force that philosophy on its own can exert. To overthrow one and replace the other requires 'practical energy', at first of a destructive kind, driven by anger and frustration, and subsequently of a productive kind, driven by hope and fervour.

The second reason why Marx thinks philosophy could not be the solution to the alienation condition is more complex. It lies in a supposed tendency of philosophy:

> [The solution of theoretical opposition] is thus by no means an exercise in epistemology but a real problem of life that philosophy could not solve because it conceived of it as a purely theoretical task. (153)

In so far as philosophy recognizes the alienation condition at all, it has a tendency to misdiagnose it as fundamentally a problem of knowledge. This is to claim that, at the root, what explains our being divided (from others, our world, our own activity and its products, and ourselves) is a matter of our having false beliefs, our being dependent on faulty mechanisms for acquiring and validating new beliefs and so on.

This is a misdiagnosis, in Marx's view, not because such problems of knowledge play *no* role in bringing about the alienation condition (he may well think they play a major role), but because they are only *part* of the explanation, and because by making us concentrate on this one part, philosophy makes us miss what *is* at the root of the explanation, the role played by work under capitalism, a factor that extends far beyond problems of knowledge, in part because it is responsible for creating the context in which such problems thrive.

If philosophy *does* tend to misdiagnose the problem in this way, it will inevitably mis-prescribe when it offers its 'remedy'. The tendency will be to suppose that, in order to solve the alienation condition, we need only correct what is false in our beliefs and improve what is faulty in our mechanisms for acquiring and validating new beliefs.

Again, the objection is not that correcting our beliefs and mechanisms plays *no* part in the remedy (Marx may well think it will play a major role) but that doing so must not be regarded as exhausting what has to be done. For these corrections may well force our economic system to adapt, but since it will leave capitalism itself in place, in some form, it must fail to root out the causes of the alienation condition, so that this condition too will survive, in some form.

(v) Summary

Communism, not philosophy, is the solution to capitalism and to the alienation condition in which capitalism places us. Marx's position has a dual aspect: his descriptive and normative projects dovetail at the most fundamental level. That capitalism is the cause and communism the remedy for the alienation condition is both the reason why communism will overthrow capitalism and the reason why it should.

When we combine Marx's analysis of the alienation condition (previous chapter) with his remedy for it (present chapter), we obtain what we might call his 'master argument'. We ought to be living in a world in which all individuals fully and freely exercise active self-realization. But by producing and sustaining the alienation condition, work under capitalism denies us this opportunity. To overthrow capitalism and remedy the alienation condition requires revolution and the institution of communism. So this is what we ought to engage in.

2. Marx and Descartes

Our interest in Marx is with how one should live and how we should organize ourselves in society. Our interest in Descartes was with what there is and how we know. Despite the fact that these are very different kinds of philosophical issue, there are two particularly significant formal similarities in the ways that Marx and Descartes handle their material. Noticing them improves our grasp and sharpens our evaluation of their arguments.

(i) Descartes, Marx and the undermining claim

As we have seen, Descartes and Marx share the strikingly optimistic thought that the bad situations they face undermine themselves. It is worth fixing more exactly the extent of the likeness here. Descartes thinks scepticism itself is the remedy for the sceptical situation because continued doubting leads to the proof of the Cogito argument, which itself provides a foundation for further knowledge, and thus a remedy for doubt and the sceptical situation to which it gave rise. Marx thinks alienation itself is the remedy for the alienation condition because continued divisiveness (between oneself and others; between parts of oneself) leads to the outbreak of revolution, which not only destroys capitalism but also replaces that economic system with communism, providing a foundation for the unification of oneself with others and with oneself, and thus a remedy for divisiveness and the alienation condition to which it gave rise. Thus both Descartes and Marx think the cause of the bad situations they face can be made their remedy; and both think this is only possible if the 'badness' is pushed far enough.

(ii) Descartes, Marx and the mirroring claim

There is also a strong formal similarity in the way that Descartes and Marx mirror analysis and remedy. The analysis describes the steps by which one descends into a bad situation; the remedy proposes the steps by which one ascends from it; and their proposal is that the one replicates the other in reverse.

Descartes descends into the sceptical situation by first doubting beliefs about what the senses tell him of objects generally, then beliefs about what the senses tell him about objects close by and in plain view, then beliefs about very simple and general things, then beliefs about

God, before finally meeting a belief about himself that doubting shows him can never be doubted, and then using this point as a foundation by which to ascend to knowledge concerning these same subjects but in reverse order: first concerning himself, then God, then very simple and general things, then what the senses tell him about objects close by and in plain view, and finally what the senses tell him about objects generally.

Marx portrays movement into the alienation condition by a similar descent, from the outer to the inner circles of alienation, from finding no satisfaction or confirmation in the products of labour, through feeling one's world is hostile to one, to finding one's work is forced on one, to feeling that one's own actions do not belong to oneself and finally to feeling that one's self is not one's own but divided against one; at which point – Marx thinks – one must revolt, and in revolt find at last an aspect of oneself with which one can truly identify, an aspect around which one can feel unified, and use this as a foundation for the pursuit of communistic change whose development ascends to unification with the same entities but in reverse order: first the sense of unity with oneself and one's own actions, then the sense that one freely chooses one's work and that one's world is one's home and finally the ability to regard what one produces as a source of satisfaction and confirmation.

We can put this formal similarity to immediate use. A considerable cause for suspicion in Descartes' programme was the fact that his ascension from doubt so exactly mirrored his descent into it. We wondered whether he had decided what *is* the case by appeal to what he *wanted* to be the case, modelling his analysis on his remedy rather than the other way round. We now have cause to wonder whether Marx is not vulnerable to the same charge for the same reason.

3. Questions

Marx proposes that the remedy for the alienation condition rests with immersion in alienation, in the divisiveness of that situation. But his optimistic audacity may be misplaced.

(i) Is communism the solution to the alienation condition?

Suppose we accept what we shall soon question: that communism *would* solve the alienation condition. We might nevertheless deny that it is *the* solution. To count as *a* solution, it would simply have to abolish the alienation condition. But this is, after all, a fairly minimal requirement. If one contemplates taking a sledgehammer to crack a nut, the fact that one *will* crack it is not the only thing worth considering. The reason why using a nutcracker instead counts as a better solution, perhaps even *the* solution, is that it is equally certain of cracking the nut, but with an exertion of force that is in proportion to the problem and in a manner that risks little if any collateral damage. And the worry about Marx's proposal is that communist revolution and the abolition of private property are neither proportionate nor risk minimizing. (Even if we accept that twentieth-century experiments in communism did not follow Marx's prescription and hence are no guide to the loss of life we may expect in the revolution that he predicted would overthrow capitalism, it is quite clear that Marx expected there to be significant loss of life and, for a considerable period, deep and universal disruption.)

Marx accepts that there is at least one alternative to communism that is not alienating (feudalism). So he will not have demonstrated that communism is *the* solution unless he can show that there is no possibility of achieving a fourth alternative (besides feudalism, capitalism and communism): an economic system that is neither exploitative nor alienating, because it gives due weight to identity, making one's productive activity depend in the right kind of way on who one is.

(ii) Is philosophy incapable of solving the alienation condition?

Marx, recall, has two reasons in play here. The first is that 'practical energy' of an extra-philosophical (destructive and then constructive) kind is required to overthrow the economic system responsible for the alienation condition. And if what we mean by 'solving the condition' is 'being sufficient of itself to overthrow the system responsible for it', Marx's premise seems unexceptionable. But we might equally (or more) reasonably be taken to mean 'showing that the system responsible for it should and will be overthrown'. And since this is precisely the achievement that Marx claims for his own philosophizing, he himself could not then endorse this premise.

Marx's second reason is that philosophy tends to misdiagnose and mis-prescribe the alienation condition as fundamentally an issue of knowledge. Suppose we accept, for the sake of argument, that philosophy does indeed prioritize problems of knowledge. Evidently, Marx did appreciate that such problems – our having false beliefs, our being dependent on faulty mechanisms for acquiring and validating new beliefs and so on – play *some* role in bringing about and sustaining the alienation condition. And it is equally plausible to insist that such problems do not play the *only* role here, if only because they need a context in which to thrive, and that context is constituted by factors that extend beyond beliefs and belief-forming mechanisms. But there is good reason to doubt that Marx attributed sufficient significance to problems of knowledge, as we shall now see. Indeed, it is one reason why his 'remedy' may fail. And since he needs to prioritize problems of knowledge, and thus appreciate the reminders and employ the resources of philosophy, this is another reason why he himself should not endorse this premise.

(iii) Is Marx's master argument sound?

Problems of knowledge combine with problems of desire when we consider the 'master' argument underlying Marx's analysis of the alienation condition and the remedy he proposes for it.

To evaluate the argument, it will be helpful to separate the premises. (1) We ought to be living in a world in which all individuals fully and freely exercise active self-realization. (2) Work under capitalism produces and sustains the alienation condition, thus denying individuals the opportunity to exercise active self-realization. (3) To overthrow capitalism and remedy the alienation condition requires revolution and the institution of communism. (4) Given (1–3, we ought to engage in revolution and institute communism.

(a) The self-defeating problem

But (1) may be too strong to be true. Indeed, it may be self-defeating to claim that we ought to be living in a world in which all individuals fully and freely exercise active self-realization.

For suppose we agree. We know that not everyone desires to exercise active self-realization. Given the opportunity, some refuse to take it up, precisely because they lack this desire. So it seems that the only way to get all individuals to exercise active self-realization is either (i) to control what they *desire* (so that they *do* want to exercise it) or (ii) to control what they *do* (so that they *exercise* it no matter what they desire). But obviously options (i) and (ii) deny individuals the opportunity to exercise themselves 'fully and freely'. So it seems that the only way to *achieve* what we want is to *prevent* what we want: that all individuals fully and freely exercise active self-realization. And it is in this sense that (1) seems self-defeating. We cannot achieve it without preventing it.

(b) The weakness problem

We might weaken (1) to escape the self-defeating problem. For example, we might narrow the set by withdrawing the insistence that *all* individuals actively self-realize. And we might change the modality by withdrawing the insistence that active self-realization be *actual*. The result – (1*) for example – might well escape the self-defeating problem:

> (1*) We ought to be living in a world in which it is possible for all who desire it to fully and freely exercise active self-realization

But there is a considerable price to weakening (1), in this or any other way. To justify revolution, with the likely loss of life and deep and universal disturbance involved, the master argument needs (1) in its original form. Substituting (1*) or any similar modified premise renders the argument as a whole too weak to entail its conclusion (4). It would not license, let alone justify, revolution.

(c) The 'real problem' and justification

Even if we leave (1) at its present strength, it is not clear that its combination with (2)–(3) is sufficient for (4). To *justify* revolution and the deep and universal changes it would bring, the alienation condition must *be* a sufficient harm.

But Marx seems to acknowledge that this condition is only a harm for some. Indeed, he acknowledges that for others it is actually a *good*: the propertied class 'finds in this self-alienation its confirmation and its good, its own power: it has in it a semblance of human existence' (*The Holy Family* p. 134).

If Marx is correct about this, it gives us two reasons to doubt his master argument. The first is a variant of the weakness problem. If some – indeed a whole class – find their *good* in the alienation condition, then that condition may not be bad *enough* to justify the revolution required to change it. The second is a new problem. If some find their good in the alienation condition, then it is perhaps not that condition itself which is the 'real' problem but rather the fact that some do *not* find in it 'a semblance of human existence'. And this would imply that Marx's whole analysis – not simply the master argument – is not focused in the right way.

(d) The 'real problem' and motivation

Even if we allow that (1)–(3) would justify (4), it is not clear that (4) would matter in the sense that Marx (rightly) insists that it *ought* to matter, that is *practically* (he sometimes gives the impression that this is the *only* sense in which it ought to matter). Set aside what would *justify* revolution and the deep and universal changes it would bring. Would (1)–(4) *motivate* people to perform the necessary actions?

Evidently, the alienation condition would have to be recognized as a sufficient harm. But, as we know, Marx acknowledges that a whole class recognize alienation for what it is, and, far from motivating them to change the status quo, it motivates them to preserve it. This is further reason to wonder whether the alienation condition is bad enough and whether Marx's analysis is properly focused. The fact that some do not find their 'semblance of human existence' in the alienation condition may be the real problem, and it may not be enough to motivate the changes required.

4. Trojan Horse syndrome

Marx is optimistic because of the dual-aspect nature of his theory of alienation. The remedy for the alienation condition is immersion rather than flight because he thinks the reason why the economic system responsible for it *should* be overthrown is the very reason why it *will* be: that it deprives us of a genuinely human existence. The same reason is supposed to ground both claims, despite the fact that one is normative and the other descriptive. His theory is supposed to bridge the gap between the normative and the descriptive. This bridge explains his optimistic audacity.

(i) Bridging the gap problem

But we may doubt whether he has indeed built this bridge. Not because capitalism *has* survived, perhaps, but because of *how* it has survived (becoming even more extreme, if we go by present radically unequal distributions of wealth). It seems to have exploited at least two major gaps left by Marx's attempt at a bridge, one to do with knowledge/belief and the other to do with desire.

The fact that work under capitalism deprives us of a genuinely human existence – if it is a fact – may be sufficient reason for the normative side of the theory. We *should* overthrow capitalism. But we may doubt whether this reason stretches to the descriptive side of the theory, spanning the distance between them. For if it is to be sufficient reason here, to assure us that capitalism *will* be overthrown, it would have to explain why sufficient numbers of people will engage in the revolution necessary to overthrow capitalism. And this is evidently not the case.

It may be a fact that capitalism deprives us of a genuinely human existence, and yet enough people do not *recognize* it is a fact; they lack the awareness, and particularly the self-awareness, to appreciate what is the case. For example, they may have false beliefs or faulty mechanisms for acquiring new ones, so they *think* they are living in a reasonable situation, or at least a situation they cannot change, even though in fact their situation is desperate and could actually be changed. Or it may be a fact that capitalism deprives us of a genuinely human existence, and enough people recognize it as such, but yet they do not *desire* active self-realization enough to engage in the revolution required to overthrow capitalism. For example, they may be risk averse and care more about the short term and have access to sufficient mind-numbing experiences, so they prefer to continue living under capitalism.

In short, nothing will change unless enough people care in the right kind of way about what they believe. It may be true that capitalism deprives us of a genuinely human existence, but if either the requisite beliefs or the requisite desires are missing from a sufficient number, capitalism will continue. And then the reason why capitalism *should* be overthrown will remain, but it will not be the reason why it *will* be overthrown – simply because there will *be* no such reason.

(ii) Root problem

So the argument in the extract does not seem cogent, and Marx's master argument faces a number of difficulties. At a deeper level, he may fail to bridge the gap between the normative and the descriptive, so his optimistic audacity is ungrounded. He himself recognized some of these difficulties, and his successors have pursued his attempts to remedy them (we shall investigate a particularly sophisticated attempt in the next chapter). But if they are successful in repairing the negative aspect of his project (that capitalism undermines itself), that leaves a problem embedded within the positive aspect (that capitalism will give way to communism).

Marx describes communism as at once a completed humanism and a completed naturalism. So how he conceives of what it is to relate humanly to things matters greatly to his positive project. As we have seen, he insists that one can only relate oneself humanly to things that relate themselves humanly to one.

This claim faces an obvious problem: the world (most of it) is quite incapable of relating itself to anything, let alone relating itself *humanly* to anything. So Marx's claim implies that we are quite incapable of relating humanly to the world.

(iii) Dividedness

In claiming that we are quite incapable of relating humanly to the world, Marx re-imposes the same absolute dividedness between oneself and the world that launched and sustained the alienation condition. He precludes the possibility of our being related to the world in the ways required to count as relating *humanly* with the world. Thus we can at best only treat the world as 'mere' animals do, as something that satisfies or resists our basic needs. At worst, the world can only be an object of indifference to us and must remain radically inaccessible to us.

But this does not quite get to the depths of the issue. These are only reached when we recall Marx's positive, communist vision. On this view, it is our *nature*, both as human beings belonging to the same species and as the particular individuals we are, to relate humanly to the world. Relating thus to the world is a necessary condition for our being able to lead properly human lives within it, and indeed for our individuals being able to lead the particular life proper to them, as the individual they are.

So it follows that, in being divided so decisively from the world, we are also decisively divided from our own selves, whose nature it is to relate humanly to the world, and thus divided also from our own activity and its products. And this, of course, is what it is to live in the alienation condition.

In short, Marx's positive project, as he himself conceives of the possibilities open to it, can only return us to the full horror of the alienation condition. This counts as the 'root' problem with his project, in part because it survives even if all the other problems we have found with it can somehow be resolved, but mainly because it brings about the downfall of the whole project.

To see this, assume for the sake of argument that Marx does succeed in demonstrating not only that capitalism *should* but also that it *will* undermine itself. The driving element of this demonstration is that capitalism nurtures and sustains the alienation condition. What we have now found is that communism also nurtures and sustains this condition. So we must conclude, by Marx's own arguments, that if communism ever does succeed in replacing capitalism, it both should and will undermine itself.

(iv) Trojan Horse syndrome

Thus Marx faces much the same Trojan Horse syndrome as Descartes and Locke. Descartes and Locke undermine their own attempts to abolish the sceptical situation by drawing insulation and detachment into the heart of their positions. Marx undermines his own attempt to abolish the alienation condition by drawing dividedness into the heart of his position. By maintaining our dividedness from the world, and hence our dividedness from our own selves, his communism plunges us back into the alienation condition just as deeply as capitalism ever did.

5. Possible paths to pursue

For Marx's early thoughts about false consciousness, dating from just before the Paris manuscripts, see his 'Towards a critique of Hegel's Philosophy of Right: Introduction' (in McLellan ed.), where he cites religion as an example. For a useful bridge between the passages discussed in this chapter and Marx's later work, read the selections from *The German Ideology* in McLellan (ed.), together with the short preface Marx wrote for his *Contribution to the Critique of Political Economy* (ibid.). For his developing presentation of communism as prediction and remedy, see *The Communist Manifesto*, published in 1848 (in McLellan ed.; sections 2–4). For his developing views on philosophy, identifying it as among the conditions of alienation from which we need to be liberated and then reflecting on the implications, see *The Poverty of Philosophy* (in McLellan ed.). For his developing analysis of life under capitalism, read the sharp and amusing section on the fetishism of commodities in *Capital* (Volume 1, chapter 1, section 4).

For the secondary literature, it might be best to begin with the short overview of Marx on ideology in Jon Elster's *An Introduction to Karl Marx* (chapter 9). Rahel Jaeggi offers an excellent overview of the concept and phenomenon of alienation in her *Alienation* (chapter 1). Michael Rosen's *Of Voluntary Servitude* (chapter 6) offers a clear and balanced account of Marx's progression towards a theory of ideology, arguing that it never quite achieved that form but moved between one and another of five 'models'. This can usefully be supplemented by G. A. Cohen's *Karl Marx's Theory of History: A Defence*, a work Rosen is most interested in weighing up (see in particular chapter 5, Cohen's precise discussion of Marx on fetishism). Jon Elster's highly critical *Making Sense of Marx* contains a fuller analysis of ideology. The discussion of 'frictionless speculations' (chapter 8) is particularly memorable. Also useful is the concluding analysis of Marx on communism and the revolution required to create it (chapter 9).

Radical IV

Analysis

How we get by

Theodor Adorno (1903–69) composed his *Minima Moralia* (1951) during and immediately after the Second World War, under conditions enforcing contemplation, as he wryly observed. He had escaped Nazi Germany, having had his right to teach revoked as a 'non-Aryan' (his father was Jewish). After a not particularly happy period in England, he moved to America and California, where he wrote what would become the book.

Minima Moralia consists of a series of interlinked short essays. Most start from an intensely private situation, often that of the cultured German émigré intellectual, and unfold to touch on issues of general relevance. It is worth bearing in mind that Adorno intended them to mark out points of attack, to provide models for future efforts of thought. So although they are intense, highly wrought pieces, they are also meant to be provisional and to provoke. Hence there are many half-humorous inversions in the titles of the essays, and the title of the book is itself a play on a work by Aristotle, which goes by its Latin name *Maxima Moralia*.

The collection as a whole is best read sparingly. Adorno allows few rays of light to pierce his gloom, but they do give dimension to his criticism. Allow too much darkness to gather, and the shape of his essays becomes indiscernible, which can make his thoughts seem monotonous and flat. Mocking Adorno for taking up residence in the 'Grand Hotel Abyss' never goes out of fashion, but few recall that Georg Lukács, who was responsible for this quip, levelled it at the German intelligentsia, not just Adorno.

Like Marx, Adorno encourages us to enter into philosophy for practical reasons. But he is also interested in what knowledge is and how we acquire it. The pressing issue for him, as for Marx, is to understand our living conditions under capitalism, to perceive what they are, what causes them and keeps them in place. But Adorno has none of Marx's striking optimism. Indeed, he often gives the impression that the best we can hope for from philosophizing is an understanding of how we get by. He is a radical philosopher, combining all the essential elements: audacious and engaged with fundamental issues that matter to us all. But he is more wary and guarded than others we have examined so far, taking his stand on analysis rather than action or experience or reason. We can detect this wariness in the sub-title of his book: *Reflections from Damaged Life*.

Minima Moralia gives reasons to doubt that the alienation condition will undermine itself. Capitalism is becoming too subtle in the way it undercuts our attempts to be genuinely self-aware, to desire appropriately, to act in committed and consistent ways. Instead, Adorno offers a more sophisticated approach, one that returns to analysis and subjects the alienation condition to the closest critical scrutiny. In so doing, he offers ways to appreciate in detail what life under the latter stages of capitalism is like, how and why we tend to be ignorant of our true interests, to care insufficiently about our self-realization, to frustrate our own actions.

1. Living under capitalism

Adorno's sophisticated approach turns on fundamental issues about knowledge and thus returns theoretical philosophizing to centre stage. This is perhaps surprising, given Adorno's indebtedness to Marx, but it is essential to his method. Indeed, Adorno demonstrates that we must look to issues of knowledge if we are to be audacious and get at the roots of issues that matter to everyone. To that end, he offers a range of smaller-scale studies of everyday life. The aim of his philosophizing is to show, in great specificity and detail, exactly what the alienation condition is like, what manifests it and what sustains it.

There is a recurrent form to each such study, with three salient features. First, Adorno picks on an apparently unifying and significance-bearing activity that continues under capitalism. One example he offers – we shall examine it – is the giving of presents. This is to bring out the fact that the alienation condition is not always overtly divisive, does not necessarily strip our lives of meaning in a flagrant way.

Second, Adorno points out how this activity is frankly a masquerade. In the example we shall examine, he shows how what passes for present-giving is not genuine present-giving. This is to argue that the activity does in fact belong to the alienation condition, that it is actually divisive, that it does strip our lives of meaning.

Third, Adorno highlights the way in which we ourselves are involved in the masquerade. In this example, Adorno shows how it suits us, for various reasons, to practice what passes as present-giving rather than the real thing. This is to force us to recognize that part of the subtlety of capitalism is the way that it co-opts us in the repression of our own ability to know and desire what is in our true interests.

Together, these three features serve Adorno's underlying aim: to show that no purely external remedy for the alienation condition will work, that the true remedy must be one that also frees us from constraints that we impose on ourselves.

(i) Under capitalism, people tend not to give presents

We are forgetting how to give presents.

Violation of the exchange principle has something nonsensical and implausible about it; here and there even children eye the giver suspiciously, as if the gift were merely a trick to sell them brushes or soap. Instead we have charity, administered beneficence, the planned plastering-over of society's visible sores. In its organized operations there is no longer room for human impulses, indeed, the gift is necessarily accompanied by humiliation through its distribution, its just allocation, in short through treatment of the recipient as an object. (46; all page references in this chapter are to Theodor Adorno's *Minima Moralia*; see the Bibliography for full details)

When people appear to be giving presents, that tends to be in appearance only. What they are actually doing is quite otherwise. To make the point, Adorno distinguishes between two sets of characteristics which – he is explicit – hold for private as well as public situations.

> Even private giving of presents has degenerated to a social function exercised with rational bad grace, careful adherence to the prescribed budget, sceptical appraisal of the other and the least possible effort. Real giving had its joy in imagining the joy of the receiver. It means choosing, expending time, going out of one's way, thinking of the other as a subject: the opposite of distraction. Just this hardly anyone is now able to do. At the best they give what they would have liked themselves, only a few degrees worse. (46)

On the one hand, Adorno identifies features that are essential to genuine present-giving: 'thinking of the other as a subject'; violating the exchange principle, acting on a 'human impulse', showing good grace, going out of one's way, making a substantial effort, choosing, expending time, finding joy in imagining the joy of the receiver. On the other hand, Adorno points out features that characterize what actually happens under capitalism, what *passes* for present-giving, which he summarizes as 'treatment of the recipient as an object': instead of acting in the ways essential to genuine present-giving, people tend to regard such actions as a trick, to prefer administering charity, to accompany distribution with humiliation, to adhere carefully to the prescribed budget, to subject the recipient to sceptical appraisal, to make the least possible effort and to treat the occasion as an opportunity for distraction.

Adorno thinks this tendency, now general, causes the capacity to act otherwise to atrophy. Genuinely to give a gift is not just something people are 'forgetting' how to do but something that 'hardly anyone is now *able* to do'.

(ii) Under capitalism, people prefer not to give presents

> The decay of giving is mirrored in the distressing invention of gift-articles, based on the assumption that one does not know what to give because one really does not want to. This merchandise is unrelated like its buyers. It was a drug in the market from the first day. (46)

Adorno pursues the analysis from outer to inner, from what people *tend* to do to what they *prefer* to do. The observation that people *tend* not to give presents might be explained as the effect of alien imposition, something that life under capitalism forces on people so that they are unable to act in any other way. But Adorno now argues that this is what people *prefer*, that this is something that meets sufficiently with their desires, so they choose to act in these ways. He uses the prevalence of various shopping gimmicks as evidence. Desire is implicated twice here by its lack: in relation to knowledge (people do not really want to *know* what to give) and to action (people do not really want to *give*). It is not just that people tend to lack these desires, but that they do not care enough to hide their lack. Indeed, Adorno treats another gimmick as evidence of a tendency to flaunt their lack:

> Likewise, the right to exchange the article, which signifies to the recipient: take this, it's all yours, do what you like with it; if you don't want it, that's all the same to me, get something else instead. Moreover, by comparison with the embarrassment caused by ordinary presents this pure fungibility represents the more human alternative, because it at least allows the receiver to give himself a present, which is admittedly in absolute contradiction to the gift. (46)

The recipient of such a 'present' has not truly been given a present. He might get himself something else, but Adorno thinks (his sarcasm aside) that to suppose he has thereby given himself a present is to misunderstand genuine present-giving, to engage in 'contradiction'.

Gift-tokens are a particularly pure form of the 'fungibility' that shopping gimmicks have realized under capitalism. But since they can usually only be exchanged for certain kinds of thing – for example one usually has to buy a book with a book token – gifts of money are perhaps the purest form of all.

(iii) In these conditions, people freeze

> Besides the greater abundance of goods within reach even of the poor, the decline of present-giving might seem immaterial, reflection on it sentimental. However, even if amidst superfluity the gift were superfluous – and this is a lie, privately as much as socially, for there is no one today for whom imagination could not discover what would delight him utterly – people who no longer gave would still be in need of giving. In them wither the irreplaceable faculties which cannot flourish in the isolated cell of pure inwardness, but only in live contact with the warmth of things. A chill descends on all they do, the kind word that remains unspoken, the consideration unexercised. (46–7)

When people tend (and prefer) to do what only *passes* for present-giving, Adorno describes them as 'freezing': they both harden and halt, ice up and become suspended.

> This chill finally recoils on those from whom it emanates. Every undistorted relationship, perhaps indeed the conciliation that is part of organic life itself, is a gift. He who through consequential logic becomes incapable of it, makes himself a thing and freezes. (47)

The passage is a little obscure, but Adorno seems to have two points in mind when he describes people as 'freezing', and both are characteristic of the alienation condition.

The first describes the effect on potential recipients of genuine gifts. They 'freeze' in the sense that they are denied goods that would otherwise have made their life significant and enjoyable. These goods consist not just of the actual object that is given but the relationship that genuine giving establishes with the donor, the sense of appreciation that comes from knowing the gift took effort and time, the sense of confirmation that comes from knowing the gift proceeded from a human impulse and was given with good grace and that special reverberance of joy which is generated by recognizing that one's joy as the recipient is a cause of joy in the donor. Adorno believes that no one is without need of goods. This is in part because he thinks 'there is no one today for whom imagination could not discover what would delight him utterly'.

The second sense of 'freezing' describes the effect on potential donors of genuine gifts. They 'freeze' in the sense that they allow their own abilities to atrophy: 'In them wither the irreplaceable faculties which cannot flourish in the isolated cell of pure inwardness, but only in live contact with the warmth of things.' The abilities Adorno has in mind are those that people exercise in genuine present-giving and which reveal the capacity to think of others as subjects: being sufficiently imaginative to choose what would please that other person, acting on a human impulse towards them and showing good grace, being capable of finding joy in the joy of that other person and so on. Retaining such abilities depends upon exercising them, and exercising them depends on having the opportunity to do so, and this opportunity depends on having 'live contact' with others. This is why Adorno claims that 'This chill finally recoils on those from whom it emanates'. If one does not exercise one's abilities for genuine present-giving, one makes oneself unavailable for, and eventually incapable of, the live contact with others on which retaining such abilities depends, and thus these abilities atrophy, so one eventually loses them and (in this second sense) 'freezes'.

Since everyone is both a potential recipient and a potential donor of genuine gifts, everyone who lives under capitalism is liable to 'freeze' in both senses, making them incapable of the kinds of relationship with others and themselves which make genuine present-giving possible. Adorno deepens the implications by describing 'every undistorted relationship' and 'the conciliation that is part of organic life itself' as themselves gifts. In becoming incapable of genuine present-giving, one is cut off from these also.

(iv) Summary

Adorno is attentive to the subtle ways that capitalism makes its alienation condition palatable. Capitalism enables what passes for present-giving to flourish. And Adorno acknowledges that genuine present-giving is a unifying and significance-bearing activity. This is why capitalism can represent life under its system as *not* dividing us from others, our world, our own activity and its products, and ourselves; as *not* depriving what we do and relate to of meaning; as *not* denying significance or value to what we are. But this is all a sham in Adorno's view. And it is not just that what capitalism enables to flourish is a masquerade rather than genuine present-giving. The real danger is that, by engaging in what merely passes for present-giving, people submit to practices that are divisive and value depriving. So although they may think, or at least tell themselves, that they are doing something unifying and significance bearing, they are in fact actively promoting the alienation condition. More specifically, not only do they deny themselves goods that would otherwise make their lives significant and enjoyable, they also allow their own abilities to atrophy in ways that divide them both from others and from themselves.

2. Wider context

(i) Smaller-scale analyses

Adorno's analysis of present-giving fits into a range of similarly sophisticated smaller-scale analyses whose conclusions combine to argue collectively as follows.

Capitalism ensures that people do not know what their true interests are. Capitalism also ensures that people do not know that their true interests cannot be met in the status quo. Hence capitalism ensures that people lack requisite *knowledge* – specifically, they do not fully know that they are alienated. Moreover, capitalism ensures that people irrationally prefer what is actually worse for them. Hence capitalism ensures that people lack requisite *desire* – specifically, they do not will what is good for them. Given that capitalism ensures that people lack requisite knowledge and desire, it is no surprise that they can and do live under the alienation condition without being motivated to change it. Hence that condition does not undermine itself.

Instead, Adorno thinks the alienation condition must be undermined by enlightening people and by emancipating them. Enlightenment ensures that people possess the requisite knowledge: that they *do* know they are alienated and complicit in this alienation. Emancipation ensures that people possess the requisite desires: that they *do* will what is good for them.

(ii) Enlightenment

Enlightenment takes the form given it by the smaller-scale analyses. We may look to other examples to make the point. Adorno offers an analysis of marriage, for example, in which he claims that, under capitalism, what we represent as a community of interests tends instead towards the degradation of all involved. Again, he offers an analysis of manifestations of virility which claims that, under capitalism, what we think of as latent violence directed towards others is at least equally self-directed. He offers an analysis of anti-capitalist movements which claims they are not immune to distortion since they also exist in conditions created by work under capitalism. In Adorno's analysis of solidarity in socialism, for example, he claims that what is represented as true brotherhood tends instead to be mere slavish confidence in the all-seeing, all-powerful Party.

The idea is that, in appreciating these ways in which we tend to delude ourselves under capitalism, we will come to know fully that (and how) we are alienated.

(iii) Emancipation

Emancipation is also dependent on smaller-scale analyses for its form. Thus Adorno offers an analysis of students of political economy under capitalism which claims that those who lack a sense of tradition – and might be expected to hate tradition – tend instead to be easily swung around, desiring instead what is established and endorsed and accepted. Again, he offers an analysis of psychoanalysis under capitalism which claims that we desire a cure for our neuroses with the aim of restoring our capacity for pleasure, when the mere concept of this, 'capacity for pleasure', threatens to devalue pleasure. And he gives an analysis of philosophizing itself which argues that, under capitalism, what philosophers tend to desire (that their claims are absolutely correct, irrefutable) is not what matters (that their claims show insight).

The idea is that, in appreciating these ways in which we tend to make bad choices under capitalism, we will come to desire what is actually in our interests, what is good for us (e.g. an end to being alienated).

(iv) Present-giving

It is clear enough how the analysis of present-giving is meant both to enlighten and to emancipate. Under capitalism, we tend to replace genuine present-giving with what passes for such and thus delude ourselves into thinking that we can unify ourselves with others in significance-bearing acts while avoiding the substantial efforts and emotional commitments required. In coming to see the distance between what is necessary for genuine present-giving and what we actually do, we come to know that (and how) we are alienated. Again, in appreciating the difference between treating another as a subject and as an object, between acting on a human impulse and merely distracting oneself, between finding joy in the joy of the recipient and sceptically appraising them so as to discover what would content them, we come to desire what is good for us, what is truly in our own interests.

(v) Adorno and Marx

Adorno differs from Marx in many ways, but two are particularly worth noting here. One has to do with the problem Marx encountered in trying to bridge the gap between the normative and the descriptive aspects of his theorizing.

The fact that capitalism is responsible for the alienation condition was supposed to explain not only why this economic system *should* be overthrown but also why it *will* be overthrown. As we saw, this assumes what need not be the case: that sufficient numbers of people both recognize that capitalism deprives us of a genuinely human existence and care enough about having such an existence to overthrow this system. And because this need not be the case, Marx's striking optimism and audacity turned out to be groundless. We cannot count on the alienation condition to undermine itself.

Now this line of criticism may seem too theoretical to be convincing or worrying. 'True', it might be said, 'we might spot gaps of this sort on paper, but they do not open up in reality; and what we are concerned with here are practical matters'. To respond, we need the kind of detail that would make the criticism seem urgent and compelling: specific facts and concrete features that embed it in everyday life.

It is detail of this kind that Adorno's smaller-scale analyses offer. And they do not merely enliven the problem, convincing us that it really is a problem. They also point the way to a remedy, a resolution. In the present-giving study, for example, it is by recovering a deep and nuanced appreciation of the distance between genuine giving and what merely passes for such that we also recover an equally rich sense of what would be required if we were to give presents in a genuinely unifying and significance-bearing way.

A second marked difference is that Adorno returns philosophy to the position from which Marx sought to exclude it. Not that Adorno gives in to the silly illusion that philosophy alone could undermine capitalism and the alienation condition to which it gives rise. But he does think that philosophy tends to diagnose this condition as fundamentally a problem of knowledge (as Marx does), and (as Marx does not) he thinks philosophy is quite correct in this.

On Adorno's view, what explains our being divided (from others, our world, our own activity and its products, and ourselves) is essentially a matter of our having false beliefs, our being dependent on faulty mechanisms for acquiring and validating new beliefs. Indeed, it is part of the alienation condition itself that we lack genuine knowledge of our condition and how to change it, that we lack the appropriate desires to change it, to engage in active self-realization. So he identifies as primary tasks the need to secure self-awareness that is genuine (in that it tracks the facts about us) and the need to encourage desiring that is appropriate (in that it tracks our true interests).

These are the needs that his smaller-scale analyses address, as we have found. They are essentially needs of knowledge, concerning what counts as 'genuine' self-awareness, what counts as 'appropriate' desiring. And Adorno thinks we cannot address these needs unless we address more fundamental questions about knowledge: in particular, what *kind* of knowledge is required to undermine the alienation condition (it does not fit the usual categories: it is not formal, nor speculative, nor purely a matter of facts about the world, empirical data, etc.), and how we are to obtain it.

So epistemology, the study of these knowledge issues, returns to the heart of the matter. And there is some measure of agreement here with Descartes (and not Locke): both attribute primary significance to theorizing about knowledge, a theorizing that philosophy is best suited to provide. Indeed, Adorno makes philosophy carry much of the burden in his attempt to counteract the alienation condition more effectively and to promote more suitable remedies for the economic system which gives rise to it.

3. Questions

The situation in which we set about evaluating Adorno's smaller-scale analyses is like one in which we assess the critical comments of a close acquaintance. It is not special pleading but just good sense to recognize this. If we do not, we will certainly miss whatever there is that might be of value here.

When we assess the critical comments of a close acquaintance., the comments that convey the criticism tend to be suggestive rather than fully argued through, less 'let me tell you how things are' than 'I may not be phrasing this quite correctly, but do you see what I'm trying to get at?' This is for good reason. For the real aim of this form of criticism is not to prove the critic right but to change the person criticized in some particular way, and change is usually only fully effective when it is in part self-change, when the person wills it. So the idea is not to bludgeon the person with criticism, to force them to accept conclusions *against* their will (doing so would only frustrate or defeat the real aim), but to act alongside and even *with* their will, to encourage them to want things to be different.

When critical comments are suggestive in this way and for these reasons, evaluation of them will depend greatly on one's attitude as the object of criticism. It will differ depending on whether or not one feels receptive to the critic, self-confident enough to take on their criticism, whether or not one is willing to fill in the gaps in the evidence, to take on the imaginative project required to see things in the different ways required, whether or not one feels like giving the other the benefit of the doubt, making an effort to put their views in the best, most charitable light.

It would be better if our attitude took the first of these alternatives. The point is not that, if we are to understand Adorno, we must assume his criticisms are correct. He may well turn out to be quite wrong when we have heard him out. But unless we listen in a way that is open to the possibility that he might be right, or at least partly right, we will lose the opportunity to be corrected, to learn, and thus improve our self-awareness, our ability to desire and act on our true interests.

(i) Do people tend and prefer not to give presents under capitalism?

What passes for present-giving often fails to come up to the high standards that Adorno claims are essential to the genuine practice. So much we may agree with, if we read his criticism with an interest in what might improve us. The prevalence of money-gifts, gift-tokens and gift-articles is only part of the evidence. But the crucial point is whether the standards Adorno sets are indeed essential for the practice to be genuine. And this we may doubt. Indeed, the fact that Adorno's argument for the view rests on a false alternative suggests this.

Adorno argues that, unless A gives presents to B in a way that treats B as a subject, A must be doing so in a way that treats B as an object, and hence that A's practice can only pass for present-giving. But if we refer to his own descriptors, we can see why this is false. Suppose A fails to make a substantial effort or acts in a mechanical way rather than on a human impulse; or suppose that the idea of B's joy is not a cause of joy to A; or suppose that A gives without good grace and even somewhat begrudges having to give to B. Only one of these features needs to hold for us to deny that, on Adorno's view of what this consists in, A treats B as a subject. But it certainly does not follow that A must thereby sink to treating B as an object, on Adorno's view of what this consists in. For A need not be using the gift as a trick, nor as an instrument to humiliate B, nor as a device to gain praise, nor as a mere excuse to distract himself, with no thought of B at all.

In short, A's way of giving presents may reflect the fact that he is both lazy and ungenerous but neither scheming nor malicious. This middle position is not simply available but captures the way many people give presents much of the time under capitalism. There is room for criticism of A, no doubt. But, crucially, one would say 'that is poor present-giving', not 'that is not present-giving at all'.

If this is correct, then what Adorno's high standards seem to describe is not what is *essential* to genuine present-giving but what is *exemplary*. Thus his evidence only implies that people under capitalism tend and prefer not to be exemplary in their giving of presents. He does not show that, under capitalism, people do not genuinely give presents at all.

(ii) Do people 'freeze' in these conditions?

If people did not genuinely give presents at all, that would be a good reason to describe both potential recipients and potential donors as 'freezing'. But suppose we question the very high threshold that Adorno places on genuine present-giving. Under capitalism, it may well be that people do not meet the high standards required for exemplary present-giving. But if what they nevertheless tend and prefer to do is genuinely give presents, in no matter how inconspicuous and unremarkable a manner, then they

do exercise their abilities for genuine present-giving and make themselves available for, and capable of, the live contact with others on which retaining such abilities depends. They are involved in unifying and significance-bearing practices. In short, people under capitalism might avoid 'freezing' if they *do* give presents but tend and prefer not to be *exemplary* about it.

(iii) Plumbing problem

It is unclear how much of a remedy Adorno's smaller-scale analyses are collectively supposed to represent. His pessimism about capitalism and our chances of undermining the alienation condition is often deep, but it fluctuates. Still, these analyses are clearly meant to point the way to a remedy, so it is reasonable to evaluate them on this score.

An extended metaphor helps. Marx thought that the alienation condition was so bad that people would overthrow the capitalist system responsible for it – like a quantity of water with considerable force behind it that would rush down a hosepipe and flood out with much energy and violence. But this is not how things turn out. Despite the great force behind the water (i.e. despite the great harms of the alienation condition), what emerges from the end of the hosepipe is a mere trickle. The reason is that the hosepipe has two large holes in it, so much of the water sprays out elsewhere, and what makes it to the end has lost its force. One of these holes is marked 'knowledge' and the other 'desire'. Though the alienation condition is sufficiently harmful to generate great force, people do not know how bad their condition is. Or if they do (if the water gets past this first hole), they do not desire what is actually in their own interests, or not enough to change their condition. So what little emerges as action (the water that gets past both holes) has been stripped of system-changing energy and violence.

(iv) Adorno's remedy

The remedy that Adorno's smaller-scale analyses offer is to close these holes, showing how bad our situation is, what is in our true interests.

Then we might expect that the whole body of water would emerge at the other end of the hosepipe, transmitting all its original force, and would thus flood out with the energy and violence Marx predicted. But there are at least two reasons to be sceptical.

One is already half-uncovered. Suppose Adorno's smaller-scale analyses follow the pattern of his study of present-giving. Then the alienation condition is not nearly as harmful as he presents it. (People are *not* 'freezing' under capitalism because they *are* genuinely giving gifts.) Indeed, perhaps it is not harmful enough to generate any real system-changing force in the first place. So assume for the sake of argument that Adorno does succeed in closing both holes, 'knowledge' and 'desire'. Nevertheless, what emerges at the end will not be energetic and radical.

The other reason to be sceptical concerns Adorno's proposed remedies, his hole-closing. The reason why philosophy returns to a central and fundamental role in Adorno's approach is that he makes that approach turn on knowledge. So suppose his analyses are wholly successful in what they attempt: not only do they discover a self-awareness that is genuine (one that tracks the facts about us and our condition) and a desiring that is appropriate (one that tracks what is truly in our best interests), but they secure these goods universally, transmitting this knowledge to everyone, or at least a sufficient majority of people. These considerations may be enough to close the 'knowledge' hole: enough people now know how bad their own condition – the alienation condition – is. But these considerations are not enough to close the 'desire' hole. Indeed, they do not even offer the right *kind* of patching to close this hole. For no matter how *deeply* one knows that it is not in one's own best interests to continue in this condition, and no matter how *many* know this, it does not follow that anyone will actually *desire* to change it, or that, if they do desire it, they will desire it *enough* to change it.

After all, consider what it is actually like to come to full realization of one's situation, how bad it is, how far from serving one's true interests. This self-awareness is at least as likely to cause action-forestalling depression as it is to motivate one to change that situation.

So assume for the sake of argument that Adorno does succeed in showing that the alienation condition is as harmful as he presents it, and that he does succeed in closing the 'knowledge' hole. Nevertheless, this leaves the 'desire' hole for much of the water to escape through. So what emerges would still not be energetic and radical enough to be system changing.

In short, we may doubt that Adorno's analyses point the way to a remedy. They do not seem to generate sufficient force for system change nor to secure the transmission of what force there is into effective action.

(v) Adaptability

But suppose that Adorno's smaller-scale analyses do succeed in closing the 'knowledge' hole. Another problem arises. This achievement is at best only temporary, given the extraordinary capacity of capitalism to adapt itself.

For example, it was once useful for capitalism to promote an inegalitarian system, encouraging the vast majority of people to believe that this system is an unchangeable natural phenomenon, something that it is useless to question because it is part of our nature, something we should uphold because it is right and proper that things should be so. Then persuasive analyses appeared, detailing the ways that capitalism thus deluded us about our condition and hid from us what is in our true interests. They argued that this inegalitarian system is actually a changeable social phenomenon, one that has come about through the development of certain social and economic forces, and hence one that can equally (be made to) disappear again.

But where these analyses managed to persuade the majority and thus close one knowledge hole, capitalism was able to open another, subverting the advance in knowledge by finding in it fresh reasons to promote the inegalitarian system. For if the majority of people now believe that an inegalitarian system is a changeable social phenomenon, this can be explained in such a way that it seems at least equally as justifiable as formerly. For example, capitalism can present the gross differences in income and wealth and status of such a society as the result of fair competition in which merit and hard work are rewarded while failure and fecklessness are punished. So the reason why we should now uphold the system as right and proper has adapted to fit current conceptions. It is precisely because the system is not now regarded as natural but as social that it becomes possible to present it as the result of a just and fair competition. Further analyses may appear, detailing the ways in which this competition is not actually just and fair. But by the time the majority has been persuaded, doubtless capitalism will have found fresh reasons to support the system that best suits its interests in whatever the majority has then come to believe.

The same adaptability can be found wherever analyses of what suits capitalism succeed in persuading the majority of people. For example, it once benefitted capitalism for people to suppose that the particular interests of bankers were actually the general interests of the whole of society. Since the majority no longer believe this is so, capitalism will doubtless find another subgroup whose particular interests it will more plausibly promote as the general interests of the whole.

And this adaptability of capitalism can be found subverting analyses of desire, not just analyses of knowledge. For example, it sometimes benefits capitalism if people irrationally prefer immediate satisfaction of lesser desires over future satisfaction of greater desires. But once this is no longer a benefit, capitalism is quite capable of persuading people of the converse (the merits and good sense of an 'austerity' programme, for example). Again, it often benefits capitalism if people are encouraged to believe that it is permissible, even laudable, to freeride on the abilities and hard work of others (it is the simple good sense of canny people who should be free to gain by the stupidity of their competitors). But again, once this is no longer a benefit, capitalism is quite capable of persuading people of the converse (it is the kind of selfish behaviour characteristic of venal benefit-scroungers).

Given the adaptability of capitalism, it seems that smaller-scale analyses of the sort that Adorno offers could only close the 'knowledge' hole for a short period. Not that this is necessarily a criticism of Adorno

himself, who seems to recognize that this is so (it is one good reason for his pessimism). But it is a problem for the kind of remedy he chooses to offer, that capitalism seems able to subvert any advance in knowledge that might threaten to undermine it.

4. Trojan Horse syndrome

Adorno improves on the negative aspect of Marx's proposals, offering detailed smaller-scale analyses of the alienation condition, how it operates, why it survives despite the harm it does. But these analyses leave in place and thus incorporate what we found to be the root problem with Marx.

(i) Dividedness

Adorno lacks the optimism of the early Marx, but they share a basic sense of what capitalism would have to give way to, were the alienation condition to be abolished: the completed humanism and completed naturalism we aspire to as human beings. And what figures centrally in their understanding of this humanism is the principle that one can only relate oneself humanly to things that relate themselves humanly to one. The problem, of course, is that the world (most of it) is quite incapable of relating itself to anything, let alone relating itself humanly to us. So, given what Adorno shares with Marx, he must accept that we are quite incapable of relating humanly to the world. And since he also agrees with Marx that it is our *nature* to relate humanly to the world, it seems he must accept that we are divided not only from the world but from our own selves. Hence both Marx and Adorno only succeed in returning us to the alienation condition, and in its direst form.

(ii) Trojan Horse syndrome

Adorno's sophisticated approach confronts capitalism with philosophy, with an epistemology that accounts for the nature and possibility of a particular kind of knowledge, with analyses of the alienation condition that manifest this knowledge, pointing back (to the distorting effects of this condition on what we believe and desire) and forward (to the remedies that correct for these effects). But his attempt to present the practice of gift-giving under capitalism as an exemplary case of the alienation condition with devastating effects on donor and recipient alike is undermined by an inflated notion of what genuine gift-giving is. The remedies he offers only address problems of knowledge, thus leaving a great gap over problems of desire. And even his remedies for knowledge problems can only be temporary since capitalism proves itself remarkably adaptable, able to subvert such advances for its own purposes.

Moreover, Adorno leaves in place Marx's dividedness, that conception of human beings as divided from the world and hence from ourselves that is embedded in the 'constructive' aspect of his proposals, the condition of completed humanism and completed naturalism to which we tend and to which capitalism will eventually give way. In these ways, Adorno undermines the very remedies he proposes, taking us deeper into the alienation condition.

So Adorno faces his own Trojan Horse syndrome. In this, he is just like Descartes, and Locke, and Marx. They each undermine their own attempts to abolish a disastrous state of affairs (the sceptical situation; the alienation condition) by drawing into the heart of their positions a commitment (to insulation; to detachment; to dividedness) which forces a return to the disastrous state of affairs.

It is striking that this same systematically self-undermining tendency arises with such different philosophers, confronting such different problems, theoretical and practical. It is not an occasional failing but a deep flaw. Is there something in philosophizing itself, or at least the radical ways of these philosophers, which lures them into it? Certainly if we are to make progress, we need to find a way of doing philosophy that resists the lure. And it would be valuable to make a start by engaging with a philosopher who engages with that lure.

5. Possible paths to pursue

The short essays of *Minima Moralia* are powerfully interlinked, but the following are particularly useful for comparison with the topics of this chapter: on marriage (I, §§1–11), virility (I, §24), solidarity in socialism (I, §31), tradition (I, §32), psychoanalysis (I, §38) and philosophizing (I, §44). Adorno wrote *Dialectic of Enlightenment* with Max Horkheimer at the same time as *Minima Moralia*; the section on 'The Culture Industry' is particularly relevant to this chapter.

Adorno is more often flatly derided from a distance than subjected to close, responsible criticism. *The Idea of a Critical Theory* by Raymond Geuss is the best available introduction to the issues Adorno grapples with. A short sharp book, it distinguishes lucidly between various senses of 'ideology' and 'false consciousness', clarifies the notion of the 'real interests' from which we are allegedly kept and distinguishes scientific theory from what is peculiar to the kind of analysis Adorno offers: 'critical theory'. Michael Rosen's *Of Voluntary Servitude* (chapter 7) is also very helpful and will be of particular value to those who have studied his previous chapter on Marx. For Adorno's complex response to Heidegger, see Peter Gordon's helpful analysis in *Adorno and Existence*. For a reliable overall account of Adorno's philosophical work, see *Adorno* by Brian O'Connor. It is worth supplementing these readings with biographical and historical material. *Adorno: A Biography* by Stefan Müller-Doohm is thorough on the man, and *The Frankfurt School* by Rolf Wiggershaus is equally exhaustive on the milieu. A much older but readable account by someone acquainted with some of the main protagonists is Martin Jay's *The Dialectical Imagination: A History of the Frankfurt School and the Institute of Social Research*. Two more opaque but influential works are *The Origin of Negative Dialectics: Theodor W. Adorno, Walter Benjamin and the Frankfurt Institute* by Susan Buck-Morss and *The Melancholy Science: An Introduction to the thought of Theodor W. Adorno* by Gillian Rose. Georg Lukács' quip about the 'Grand Hotel Abyss' occurs in his 1962 preface to *The Theory of the Novel*.

Radical V

Self-Criticism

7

How we might re-enter philosophy

Martin Heidegger (1888–1976) wrote *Being and Time* while being overworked as an adjunct professor at the University of Marburg. The great variety of lecture-courses he taught there enabled him to refine a familiarity with a considerable range of philosophy, from Aristotle and Aquinas to the concept of time and the metaphysical foundations of logic. This gives his book a rare combination of unity and breadth of reference, organizing an enormous variety of philosophical themes under a few leading ideas.

Being and Time received considerable acclaim when it appeared in 1927. It gained Heidegger extraordinary prominence in Germany and helped secure him the coveted chair in philosophy at Freiburg, from which his old teacher Edmund Husserl retired in 1928. It also laid the foundations for his international reputation and remains the work for which Heidegger is best known. To what extent it is compromised by fascist ideology – it was published several years before his appalling involvement with the Nazi party – is an important issue for scholarship.

Approaching *Being and Time* for the first time can be daunting, so it is as well to know that Heidegger himself was daunted. He set out to write a two-part work with three divisions in each part but only ever completed the first two of these six divisions. It is also worth recognizing that there is a degree of tension and inconsistency even in what he did complete. There is then good reason not be overawed by the book. It is best treated as a work under process of construction – unsure of its final form, constantly revising its own aims, insecure about its methods, uncertain of its findings – rather than a timeless repository of settled conclusions.

The problems Heidegger raises are much the same as those we have been puzzling over. What is our nature, as minded beings? How are we related to the material world? What can we know for certain, and how? What do we need in order to live a genuinely human existence? How should we cope with our present living conditions? How and why do we mislead ourselves about what is in our best interests? So our journey to this point has put us in touch with Heidegger, able to wrestle with what he wrestles with.

Indeed, the correspondence goes deeper, for Heidegger also recognizes our underlying puzzle: that philosophers tend to undermine their own efforts, to embed themselves ever more deeply in the very problems they are trying to solve. We have asked whether there is something in philosophizing itself, or the way philosophers tend to philosophize, that creates this Trojan Horse syndrome. And Heidegger not only addresses this question but also offers an answer. He spots what he claims is a catastrophic flaw at the heart of previous philosophizing: it neglects its proper task, without which there is no genuine philosophizing. If he is right, this might well explain why previous attempts at philosophy undermine their own efforts.

This overview gives the impression that Heidegger's project is fundamentally negative. Not so. His attempts to overcome philosophy's fundamental flaw enable him to re-open our old questions by pursuing new ones. So we shall investigate the three that concern him most in three successive chapters. What grounds our everyday ways of living in the world? Is it possible for us to live in an authentic way? And how should we face our own death? In his answers, Heidegger reveals himself to be a model radical philosopher, combining all the essential elements: audacious and engaged with fundamental issues that matter to us all about how the world is and how we should live in it. But this is a very uneasy, self-questioning form of the urge to be radical, one that takes its stand not on reason or experience or action or even analysis but on self-criticism.

1. Re-entering philosophy

Being and Time is hard to read. The style is difficult, the approach disorientating, the argument sunk deep in exotic terminology. It would not only be daft to deny this but seriously misguided, for these obstacles are fully intended and have a clear purpose. Understanding why Heidegger imposes considerable inconvenience on the reader gets us to the heart of the matter.

(i) Difficulty

Suppose philosophy is like a nut that has been forced incorrectly onto a bolt. The thread has been fouled up and, in places, lost. Getting the nut off again requires twisting it all the way back to the beginning, which means making exactly the same series of right and wrong moves that threaded it onto the bolt in the first place, coaxing it over the distorted ridges, and all in reverse. Then one has to start afresh, cutting an entirely new thread with the nut, and this time doing so in a sufficiently alert and attentive manner, making sure to keep the groove straight and true.

Philosophy requires this kind of re-entry work, Heidegger believes. We need to refashion the questions and concepts and modes of inquiry that have been used to drive and guide philosophy, turning it back through the right and wrong moves that led to its distortion, so that when we re-direct philosophy into the route of a sound investigation, one that fulfils the essential tasks of philosophy, we will be using concepts, addressing questions and deploying modes of inquiry that are fit for the purpose.

So it is no good ignoring the difficulties of reading Heidegger and relying instead on an accessible paraphrase. What would make it accessible would be the fact that it would deploy the familiar old questions and concepts and modes of inquiry, the very ones that had got us jammed in the first place. But it is not only the introduction of new features that makes Heidegger's writing difficult. It is also his studied attempt to keep the reader wary and vigilant so that we do not fall back into the old grooves. In short, if we want to grasp his argument, we simply have to work with and through the difficulties his writing presents.

(ii) History

Whether this justification succeeds must depend, of course, on its starting-point. Has philosophy indeed been distorted, like a nut forced incorrectly onto a bolt? That may seem implausible. After all, previous philosophy has taken profoundly different forms, investigated profoundly different sorts of issue, theoretical and practical. Is it really plausible to think that *all* philosophy has gone much the same – wrong – way?

To appreciate Heidegger's answer, it helps to recall salient features of the journey we have made to this point, and particularly what previous philosophers say about the really deep and revealing issues – what philosophy is, why it is worth doing, what it can do, what it should do, how we should best set about doing it.

Descartes gives philosophy a foundational role. He makes the search for truth the search for foundational principles of knowledge of which the individual is certain and from which they can deduce other truths. These principles decide whether individuals are correct to believe what experience tells them. Experience cannot provide these foundational principles, nor can science, the systematic investigator of experience. But reason is capable of providing these foundational principles and of deciding whether the individual is correct to hold them. And this gives philosophy its foundational role, as the systematic investigator of reason. It is up to philosophy to find and secure these principles. The philosopher is like an architect, drawing up the plan according to which science builds.

Locke, on the other hand, regards experience alone as the ultimate source of knowledge and hence of any principles on which particular knowledge is based. This gives science, as the systematic investigator of experience, the foundational role. Science, not philosophy, provides the principles on which particular knowledge is based. By clarifying ambiguity about the meaning of terms and pointing out fallacies in arguments, philosophy's task is to clear the way for science. The philosopher is essentially a servant of science, an 'underlabourer', as Locke himself puts it.

Marx differs from either. He uses philosophy to help understand capitalism but recognizes that the harms of this system can only be dealt with by radical change. Such change will come through frustration with current conditions. Philosophy can be helpful in revealing these conditions, but it has a tendency to recast all problems in a form for which philosophy can be the unique solution. For example, it tends to explain the capacity of capitalism to harm in terms of those problems of knowledge that it is best placed to resolve. To some extent, then, philosophy tends to misunderstand itself and what it can offer, and so needs constantly to be corrected.

Adorno differs again. He thinks the harms of capitalism are possible because of its capacity to subvert and undermine our ability to know our condition and to know what is in our best interests. To that extent, these harms are in a form for which philosophy is in the best place to resolve them. These harms need to be understood in detail if they are to be resisted. The task for philosophy is to analyse facts about the world, empirical data, and draw conclusions from it about what our true condition is and what it is in our best interests to do.

Clearly then, the philosophers we have been examining disagree profoundly about the deep questions – what philosophy is, why it is worth doing and so on. But we have also seen they have more fundamental features in common. For example, we have found that (a) they all tend to undermine their own efforts, thus failing to achieve the philosophical assurance they seek. Moreover, we have found that what explains why their proposals undermine their own remedies is that (b) they all tend to present minded beings, like us, as essentially 'insulated' or 'detached' or 'divided' from the world. Is there something that might explain this commonality?

(iii) The question

Heidegger thinks so and gives a taste of his view at the very start of *Being and Time*:

> Do we in our time have an answer to the question of what we really mean by the word 'being'? Not at all. So it is fitting that we should raise anew *the question of the meaning of Being*. (1; all page references in this

chapter are to Martin Heidegger's *Being and Time;* see the Bibliography
for full details)

Previous philosophers, according to Heidegger, fail to give proper
consideration to 'Being' – being in general, that which is shared by
everything that is, at the most fundamental level. Indeed, he thinks
they do not even really raise the question of what 'Being' means,
what its proper significance is. And this has immediate consequences,
Heidegger thinks. For this is the first issue that philosophy must face.
To ignore it as previous philosophers do, who set out to form views of
particular beings or particular kinds of being, is to duck the primary
philosophical task. And by missing out the first stage in philosophizing,
they condemn their researches to falsity and distortion. For we will not
know the right way to think about particular beings until we know how
to think about Being in general.

Evidence of the disaster is plain to see, Heidegger thinks. By
overlooking the basic question for philosophy, previous philosophers
inevitably misrepresent and distort the particular beings we are. For
example, there is a consistent tendency to present us as minded beings
that are essentially 'insulated' or 'detached' or 'divided' from the world.
This is a deep misrepresentation, Heidegger thinks. And it is only
possible because the philosophers responsible have tried to miss out
the first stage in philosophizing.

If Heidegger is right, we have an answer to our puzzle. How could
it be that all previous philosophy fails, despite taking such profoundly
different forms? Because previous philosophers share common features
and underlying reasons which mean, in each case, that (c) failing to
raise the question of the meaning of Being leads to (b) misrepresenting
particular beings which leads in turn to (a) undermining their own
efforts.

But the implications go deeper still. For Heidegger argues that raising
'the question of the meaning of Being' is philosophy's proper task. If
that is correct, then it is something essential for philosophy, without
which one would not actually be philosophizing at all. So the systematic

failure to raise the question of the meaning of Being is not simply a cause of local error but a blanket catastrophe for the discipline. That is why Heidegger regards previous philosophy as fatally compromised, like a nut forced incorrectly onto a bolt. And that is what justifies him in working us so hard when he attempts to re-enter philosophy.

(iv) Optimism

All this may strike one as doom-laden, and indeed there is much pessimism in Heidegger, as we shall see. But the quoted passage continues in a more optimistic vein:

> So first of all we must reawaken an understanding for the meaning of this question [the question of the meaning of Being]. Our aim in the following treatise is to work out the question of the meaning of Being and to do so concretely. (1)

Indeed, once we spell out the relevant details, Heidegger has just as much reason to be optimistic and audacious as Descartes and Marx. Descartes thinks that, finding ourselves already doubting, if we really plumb to the depths of that situation, we should come to individualistic certainty. Marx thinks that, finding ourselves already alienated, if society really experiences that condition to the full, we should come to communism. Heidegger is in a formally similar position. He thinks that, finding ourselves the sort of beings we are, if we really allow ourselves to be attentive to that being, we will re-enter philosophy in a way that does what is essential.

How so? Because of the way three claims conjoin. The first is about the task facing us, and we already know it: that the essential task of philosophy is to raise the question of the meaning of Being.

The second is about the method for carrying out this task. Heidegger advocates phenomenology, which he explains by appeal to the word's etymology. Phenomen-ology is a 'logos' (means of inquiry) rooted in confrontation with 'phenomena' (the totality of what shows itself). We carry out this inquiry when we

> let that which shows itself be seen from itself in the very way in which
> it shows itself from itself (34)

This may seem a simple matter: just letting things show themselves. But
it is difficult for at least two reasons: the temptation to get in the way
and the fact that some things show themselves in a distorted way, while
others are not able to show themselves at all, being concealed. Hence
Heidegger sees his major task as to un-distort and un-conceal. And
what taxes him most will come as no surprise: philosophy itself, and
particularly the distortions and concealments which previous attempts
at philosophy have generated. Once these impediments have been dealt
with, the idea is to lead phenomenological apprehension of a being
back to understand the Being of this being. That is how the first and
second claims link up.

The third claim is about those carrying out this task, ourselves.
Heidegger thinks there are not just different beings and different kinds
of beings, but that Being itself has different kinds. This may seem
offputtingly abstruse, but for Heidegger it reflects a perfectly mundane
practice of classifying the world that we pick up in childhood without
any metaphysical speculation: saying of some things 'who is that?' and
of other things 'what is that?' Being which belongs to something we use
'who' about differs from that which belongs to something we use 'what'
about. Being of the former sort Heidegger calls 'Dasein'. And he picks
out one crucial feature of this kind of Being: Dasein is the kind of Being
for whom Being itself is always and already in question:

> Being is that which is an issue for every such entity. (42)

It is because of this that Heidegger has cause for audacious optimism.
Suppose we agree that (i) the proper task of philosophy is to raise the
question of the meaning of Being, (ii) we require the phenomenological
method to perform this task, which is 'to let that which shows itself be
seen from itself in the very way in which it shows itself from itself', and
(iii) as Dasein, we are such that Being is always and already in question
for us. Then it follows that (iv) as Dasein, we are the appropriate point
of access for philosophy. Being is always already in question for us, after

all. So the issue of its meaning is necessarily raised whenever we let what shows itself about our own Being be seen from itself in the very way in which it shows itself from itself. Philosophy's task and method blend perfectly in us, as Dasein. Hence we ought to design our philosophical inquiry around what shows itself in us, letting it be seen from us, in the way it shows itself from us. That is what is meant by (iv) and the phrase 'point of access'. Hence the cause for audacious optimism: just letting what thus shows itself be seen from itself like this is to re-enter philosophy in a way that does what is proper and essential for philosophy.

2. Dasein

'We are ourselves the entities to be analysed' (41). This is how Heidegger introduces what he calls his 'analytic' of Dasein. And it is as well to be prepared: he works us hard with this key notion.

'Dasein' is an ordinary and everyday word (the German for 'existence'), but Heidegger uses it in an extraordinary and peculiar way. This forces even the native reader into constant alertness, asking intermittently what exactly it is supposed to mean. But the aim is sharper than this. The phenomena for which the word stands are equally ordinary and everyday, so there is a tendency for significant details to hide in plain sight. This is an impediment to phenomenology: what shows itself is not being seen. So Heidegger tries to overcome our familiarity by using extraordinary and peculiar ways to refer to phenomena. The weirdness stimulates us who are 'native' to the phenomena to notice what might otherwise be slumped, submerged in everydayness. We become more constantly alert, more attentive to what shows itself.

We can start with what we know of Heidegger's analysis and build up from there:

(i) Who

Dasein is the kind of Being that belongs to those we use 'who' about – rather than 'what'.

We use 'who' about human beings, of course, and our focus remains with them. But the concept 'Dasein' is not equivalent to the concept 'human being'. We use 'who' about beings that are not human; if there were angels or Martians, for example, we would use 'who' of them. More generally, 'Dasein' is not a biological, or psychological, or anthropological concept as 'human being' is.

(ii) In question

Dasein is the kind of Being for whom Being itself is always and already in question. If there were angels or Martians, this might be true of them also. This puts Dasein into an intimate relation with the analysis being pursued.

(iii) Understanding

Dasein is the kind of Being which

> in its very being, comports itself understandingly towards that being. (53).

If so, then Dasein is not only in a most *intimate* relation with the analysis being pursued but in a most *advantageous* relation. It is one thing to claim that we should analyse ourselves if we wish to re-enter philosophy in a way that does what is essential for philosophy. It is quite another to claim that, by making ourselves the object of our analysis, we will be investigating something to which we are already 'understandingly comported'. Quite what Heidegger means by this we shall investigate below. But it certainly seems to give him further reason to be optimistic and audacious.

(iv) Existence

Dasein is the kind of Being which exists. This may strike one as odd. Cannot the same be said of the kind of Being which belongs to those we use 'what' about – a table, a house, a tree, to use Heidegger's examples? A clue lies in the fact that Heidegger draws this feature of Dasein out of (iii):

> Dasein is an entity which, in its very being, comports itself unders-
> tandingly towards that Being. In saying this, we are calling attention to
> the formal concept of existence. Dasein exists. (53)

Heidegger is using 'exist' in a peculiar way, and he is quite explicit
about this (42). To exist is not simply to be, but to be a certain way,
indeed to enjoy that mode of Being which he calls Dasein. And there
is a philosophical point behind the licence to give special meaning to
ordinary terms. What marks out those things that exist, in this restricted
sense, is their ability to comport themselves understandingly towards
their Being. This ability is exclusive to Dasein.

(v) Da-Sein

Dasein is the kind of Being which belongs to those for whom Being
is always and already *there*. We might also say it belongs to those for
whom Being is always and already situated or located, or to be found,
so long as we use these terms – for the moment – in the most general,
schematic sense. Phenomenology reveals this, Heidegger thinks,
and etymology captures it. For the word 'Dasein' can be viewed as
a compound of two other words, 'Da' (meaning 'there') and 'Sein'
(meaning 'to be'). This Being (*Sein*) is such as to be always and already
there (*Da*).

The union within the one word 'Dasein' is as important as the
significance of its compound terms. If we see what shows itself from itself
in the very way in which it shows itself from itself, Heidegger thinks,
we will appreciate that the phenomenon around which inquiry is being
organized is a kind of *Being* that is always already *there*. But in Dasein,
this Being and its there-ness express a single unitary phenomenon. As
Heidegger sometimes puts it, the Being of Dasein belongs to its there-
ness, and its there-ness belongs to its Being.

These thoughts are undoubtedly obscure. If we set them aside for
a moment, to register the other essential features of Dasein, we may
return with greater clarity.

(vi) Mineness

Dasein is the kind of Being which belongs to those for whom Being is always and already *mine*.

> Dasein is an entity which in each case I myself am. Mineness belongs
> to any existent Dasein, and belongs to it as the condition which makes
> authenticity and inauthenticity possible. (53)

What this means for Heidegger can best be seen by putting the emphasis in different places.

Dasein is the Being *I myself* am. This reflects one crucial aspect of Dasein: that it is the kind of Being which belongs to individuals, and to individuals capable of thinking of themselves in first-person terms. So it is important to reconfigure the earlier claims in these terms: being Dasein, I find myself a 'who', in question, to whom I am comported understandingly, which exists and which is there. Heidegger is profoundly unlike Descartes, as we can already begin to appreciate. But it is worth storing away what may appear to be a formal similarity: where Descartes feels entitled to say 'I am thinking, therefore I exist', Heidegger feels equally entitled to say 'I am comporting myself understandingly towards my Being, therefore I exist'.

Dasein is the Being I myself *am*. This reflects the fact, whose significance we will explore, that Dasein is not the kind of Being which we *have*, as if it were a property or quality of something that exists anyway, still less a property I have in virtue of being something else, like being a human being (it is significant that Dasein is not to be regarded as necessarily an exclusively human phenomenon), but is something we *are*.

Finally, Dasein is the Being *I myself am*. This reflects the fact that the analysis of Dasein is crucial to our understanding of authenticity and inauthenticity. Being authentic, according to Heidegger, has to do with what is one's own. Indeed – in a phrase he often uses – it has to do with what is 'ownmost' (*eigenst*) to one. This may seem a rather formal and abstract analysis, and indeed it is, for good reason as we shall see. But Heidegger gives it deep practical significance, as we shall appreciate in the next chapter.

(vii) Being-in-the-world

Dasein is the kind of Being that realizes itself in Being-in-the-world. This also is a difficult notion, but it will throw a little – much-needed – light on the earlier claim that Dasein is the kind of Being that belongs to those for whom Being is always and already *there*.

It is significant that Heidegger draws us on towards Being-in-the-world by appeal to what we have just encountered: authenticity and inauthenticity. He describes them as 'ways in which Dasein's Being takes on a definite character' and then continues,

> they must be seen and understood a priori as grounded upon that state of Being which we have called 'Being-in-the-world'. An interpretation of this constitutive state is needed if we are to set up our analytic of Dasein correctly. (53)

The idea seems to be this. Experience shows us that we can live in various ways, where some of these comparatively superficial modes of being are proper to our Being as Dasein and some are not. And if we just think about this – without need to be justified by experience, hence a priori – we will come to appreciate that these comparatively superficial possibilities would not be available to us unless a deeper possibility were made available to us by our Being as Dasein: namely, our 'Being-in-the-world'.

In Being-in-the-world, Being and there-ness form a unity:

> The compound expression 'Being-in-the-world' indicates in the very way we have coined it, that it stands for a unitary phenomenon. This primary datum must be seen as a whole. (53)

Our Being and our world are not truly separable, even notionally. They form a single unity.

Heidegger is aware of a particular trap here: that the phrase 'being-in' in 'Being-in-the-world' might suggest that our Being and our world are to be thought of as two separate things, one existing in the other, like an object in a container. This would be wrong: one can focus on one or other, perhaps, but they remain aspects of the same 'unitary phenomenon':

> Being-in is not a 'property' which Dasein sometimes has and sometimes does not have, and without which it could be just as well as it could with it. It is not the case that man 'is' and then has, by way of an extra, a relationship-of-being towards the 'world' – a world with which he provides himself occasionally. [. . .] Taking up relationships towards the world is possible only because Dasein, as Being-in-the-world, is as it is. (57)

Heidegger avoids other terms which are similar traps. If we talk of 'minds', for example, it is difficult to resist a picture in which this one separate kind of 'thing' is related to another separate kind of 'thing', the world. The unfamiliar talk of 'Dasein' and 'Being-in-the-world' keeps us open to the possibility that what we are dealing with are not two separate kinds of thing that need to be brought into relation but a unitary phenomenon.

(viii) Unitary phenomenon

Dasein is the kind of Being whose realization as Being-in-the-world marks a unitary phenomenon. Talk of 'a unitary phenomenon' might mean several different things, of course. What is Heidegger getting at? Analogies help.

In one sense, the morning star and the evening star are a unitary phenomenon: we have two different names for the same object. But if this means we could simply replace the one with the other, this is not a good model for 'Being-in-the-world'. For Heidegger retains a use for each component term, our Being and our world. He attends selectively to one rather than the other and considers the implications of each.

In another sense, hydrogen and oxygen form a unitary phenomenon, water. But this is not a good model either. True, it is not possible to remove the hydrogen and still have water, just as it is not possible to remove our world and still have Being-in-the-world. But it is possible to remove the hydrogen and still have oxygen, whereas it is not possible to remove our world and still have the kind of Being that is at issue here.

There is a closer analogy with the essential features of a triangle. 'Being a closed figure with exactly three sides' and 'being a closed figure with exactly three angles' name two sets of properties, not mere synonyms, and we retain a use for each description. We can attend selectively to angles and their degrees rather than to sides and their lengths, and distinguish carefully between the implications of each. But we will lack proper understanding of triangles, and indeed of either description, if we do not appreciate that one cannot remove the closed figure with exactly three sides without removing the closed figure with exactly three angles. That is a rough analogy only, but it is not unlike what Heidegger means when he says Being-in-the-world is a unitary phenomenon.

3. Implications

Heidegger's analysis of Dasein is fundamental in its purpose, engaged in its design and audacious in its optimism. It is the analysis of a radical. Not the least aspect of his urge to be radical is the distance Heidegger places between himself and previous philosophers. This is partly a matter of agenda. He identifies the primary and essential task of philosophy with one previous philosophers tend to overlook: raising the question of the meaning of Being. It is also a question of technique. He uses phenomenology to replace the methods of previous philosophers because they fail to let what shows itself be seen from itself. It is partly also a question of style. His writing is intentionally difficult, partly to counteract the tendency of previous philosophers to overlook their essential task, partly to sustain the phenomenological method, keeping us alert and fully attentive to phenomena that otherwise lie distorted or concealed, and partly to express adequately what shows itself when it is seen from itself. But it is mainly a matter of conclusions. For what phenomenology uncovers is the extent to which previous philosophy has distorted or concealed the fundamental reality of things.

If Heidegger is right, we are not genuinely at risk of being 'insulated' from the world, or 'detached' from it, or 'divided' from it. The sceptical situation is only a threat if we think of each of us, and the world, as separate elements that need to be brought into relation with each other. But this cannot be so if our Being is Dasein, whose many possible ways of existing are always and already grounded in a unitary phenomenon, one that can only adequately be expressed – however exotically – by the hyphenated phrase 'Being-in-the-world'. It certainly cannot be so if we are indeed related *understandingly* to our Being. For then the sceptical situation ought not to be considered a distant possibility for us, let alone a live threat, still less something against which we need to seek *philosophical* assurance. It would be particularly dangerous to look for such assurance from forms of philosophy that neglect the one essential task of philosophy, to raise the question of the meaning of being. And it would be particularly harmful that previous philosophers represent themselves as having *found* such assurance, in the method of doubt, for example, or in empiricism.

(i) Mind

If previous philosophers have been so wrong, why have they won such acceptance? That is a good question, one that Heidegger must answer to win conviction for his own view. And he does offer explanations.

One is that previous philosophers have been able to rely on forms of language and habits of thought that imply that having a mind, or being minded, is being endowed with a thing – as if having a mind were like having a gun, or as if being minded were like being armed. Such forms and habits encourage us to think that saying 'the mind is in the world' is like saying 'the gun is in the holster'. And this in turn encourages us to consider the possibility that, just as the gun can exist outside or without the holster, so the mind might exist without the world, or at least be 'insulated' from it, 'detached' from it, 'divided' from it. It is then not surprising that previous philosophers should have taken on the task of bringing mind and world back together again, contriving ways to relate them, to overcome what insulates, detaches or divides them.

Of course, we could equally well think of being minded as being like being amusing, a way of being in the world, where the possibility of this alternative means we are not obliged to think of it in the first way. But Heidegger goes further. His claim is that, if we do raise the question of the meaning of Being, this is how we *should* think about being minded. And this disrupts the earlier progression of thought. It is open to us to think that 'mind' and 'world' name aspects of a single unitary phenomenon, one that enables us to think that saying 'the mind is in the world' is like saying 'the joking is in progress', which closes off the possibility of our thinking of a mind that exists without a world (or 'insulated', 'detached', 'divided' from the world), just as it makes no sense to think of a joking that is going on without its being in progress.

(ii) World

Another explanation Heidegger offers concerns our conception of the world. He thinks previous philosophers have been able to rely on exclusive appeal to a scientific conception: the world is conceived of as that which science can explain, particularly physics, where the explanation will appeal to causal-mechanical forces. It is then possible for former philosophers to insist that the mind cannot be explained by appeal to such forces and thus is to be conceived of as outside the world – 'insulated', 'detached', 'divided' from it. And, again, it is then easy to see why previous philosophers should be so concerned to bring mind and world together again.

Of course, it is perfectly open to us to conceive the world in this way. But we need not do so, and Heidegger thinks we should not do so if our task is to raise the question of the meaning of Being. For that task requires a particular method, which is to let what shows itself be seen from itself. And if we see the world as it shows itself from itself, Heidegger thinks, it is not as science conceives it to be. This again disrupts the earlier progression of thought. Whether or not we think the mind is to be explained by appeal to causal-mechanical forces, there is now no reason to conceive it as outside the world, or 'insulated', 'detached', 'divided' from it.

How then does the world show itself? In various ways, but Heidegger attaches clear priority to its practical, everyday aspect. In everyday Being-in-the-world, we are engaged with interacting practically with the world, relating to people, employing objects, performing actions, with a view to carrying out our tasks or desires, meeting our goals. This world is predominantly made up of what presents itself as *useful* to us, given these various tasks, desires, goals.

The locution 'in the world' needs care, but Heidegger uses it – indeed, gives it central significance in 'Being-in-the-world'. He can also speak of 'placing' minded beings in the world. For him, to *be* minded is to be a certain *way* in-the-world, and hence always already to be-in-the-world. He can even use the phrase 'having a mind', understanding it in terms of 'being minded'.

(iii) Authenticity

How bad is it to pursue philosophy as previous philosophers have done? Very bad indeed, if we press the elements of Heidegger's position together. It is not simply wrong but inauthentic to pursue a philosophy that implies our 'insulation' or 'detachment' or 'dividedness' from the world.

For suppose it is proper to us to be related understandingly towards our Being, and to be so related is (at least) to recognize that we are *there* in the world, grounded in the unitary phenomenon Being-in-the-world. Then it seems to follow that we are failing to be what is ownmost about ourselves if we deny this or seek philosophical assurance for it. And to fail to be what is ownmost about ourselves is to be inauthentic.

What grounds our existence, making it possible for us to exist in whatever way – to take on Descartes' project of doubting everything, for example – is a unitary phenomenon to which we are understandingly related: that we are always and already Being-in-the-world. We might try to imagine what it would be like if this were not the case. But we cannot believe that it is not the case and be what is ownmost about ourselves.

We will pick up these implications in the next chapter.

4. Questions

Set to one side, for a moment, the details of Heidegger's analysis of Dasein. A basic concern must have been growing. It may seem that his analysis consists of a series of assertions without argument. The sceptical situation might not be a threat if his analysis holds. But does he *show* that our Being as Dasein is grounded in the unitary phenomenon of Being-in-the-world? It is unclear why we should believe this. Is Heidegger merely defining his way out of a problem rather than resolving it?

This question is our focus because, unless he can satisfy us on this score, Heidegger has no resolution to offer and we are absolved from the need to scrutinize his secondary phenomenological findings. If Heidegger *does* have an answer, we need to see if it comes at a cost – whether, for example, it weakens the stance he is able to take towards these secondary findings. Then we will know how best to approach these details.

(i) What are we shown?

Heidegger does indeed offer a series of assertions. But can we extract more from his analysis than this? What we need, we may insist, is to be *shown* that our Being is grounded in a unitary phenomenon, Being-in-the-world. Otherwise, Heidegger will have achieved nothing more in saying 'our being is grounded in a unitary phenomenon' than the person who says 'unicorns have a horn'. This may be taken as true, despite the fact that unicorns do not even exist, for it is simply following out the way 'unicorn' has been defined.

Heidegger evidently has something of a different order of substantiality in mind: that there really is something that fits the description 'unitary phenomenon, Being-in-the-world' and that it corresponds to us in the right way to count as that in which our Being is grounded. But if he is not merely introducing a term and defining it, what *is* he doing?

We might expect the response: 'We *are* shown this; it is what the phenomenological method reveals.' But, perhaps surprisingly, this is not a response on which Heidegger seems content to rely. The assertions we have quoted concerning Dasein and Being-in-the-world occur in the introductory parts of his investigation. He is still describing what a properly directed philosophical inquiry would investigate. He is advocating the notion of a phenomenological method, not – or at least not obviously – pursuing such a method, still less achieving fundamental results by it. Whether or not the assertions about Dasein and Being-in-the-world are confirmed by subsequent applications of this method, we seem to be being allowed to suppose that they need not be arrived in this way. So what can Heidegger say in support of these claims and without applying this method?

The weakest response would be to point out that, if Heidegger simply defines his way *out* of the problems associated with the sceptical situation, then previous philosophers might equally be described as defining their way *into* these problems. For if Heidegger does not show that our Being is grounded is a unitary phenomenon, Being-in-the-world, previous philosophers do not show that our Being and the world are separate elements that need to be brought into relation with each other.

This response is the weakest available because it is *ad hominem*; even if it succeeds, it only succeeds against certain specific opponents. A stronger response follows the route we have been outlining throughout the book. We know, given their common starting-point, that previous philosophers end up with proposals that are endemically self-defeating. So it is reasonable to suppose that the problem lies with the common starting-point. This might give us reason to swap what they commonly assume as their starting-point – that our Being and the world are separate elements – for the idea that these things form a unitary phenomenon, Being-in-the-world.

(ii) Ducking the question?

If Heidegger takes this route, it may still seem that he is ducking the issue, not *showing* that our Being is grounded in a unitary phenomenon, Being-in-the-world. Not that ducking questions is always inexcusable. The ancient historian who is asked 'What are the causes of the First World War?' may reply 'That is not my area', just as the mathematician who is asked '*Why* are there numbers?' may reply 'That is not for mathematics to determine'. But Heidegger cannot excuse himself in these ways, not if philosophy is as he defines it. For as a philosopher, hence someone required to raise the question of the meaning of Being, it is precisely his task to deal with the claim at issue, that our Being is grounded in the unitary phenomenon.

Ducking questions is sometimes not merely excusable but fully justifiable. If one is asked 'Why are women more intelligent than men?', for example, there is a hidden false premise behind the question which justifies one in declining to answer it. Or again, if one is asked 'What are men *for*?' one might justifiably refuse to answer because it is uncertain what is being asked, because it is unclear what an answer would look like, or whether indeed the question has an answer. But again Heidegger cannot justify himself in these ways. The claim that our being is grounded in a unitary phenomenon does not rest on a false assumption, in his view, and he thinks it is an answer to a sufficiently determinate question: 'On what is our being grounded?'

Again, some questions can be ducked without this being exactly excusable or justifiable. If someone asks 'Why are there round squares?' or 'Why are all aunts women?' we might take our immediate task to be correcting the questioner, showing that the question only arises because there is something they are wrong about, or something they are missing. But Heidegger cannot give this response either. He is not claiming that it is solely in virtue of the meaning of the terms that our Being is grounded in a unitary phenomenon, that someone who denies or questions this must be missing semantic information.

(iii) Showing that, showing how?

A response of a different order would start by noting that the demand to *show* that our Being is grounded in a unitary phenomenon could mean either (a) showing *that* this is so or (b) showing *how* this is so. It might then claim that (a) is unnecessary, and perhaps even impossible, whereas (b) is something that Heidegger achieves, and that this is sufficient to answer our basic concern.

(a) would be unnecessary if, as Heidegger seems to suppose, our being grounded in a unitary phenomenon, Being-in-the-world, is a 'default' claim. For a default claim is one that we are licensed to hold, unless and until we are shown otherwise. And (a) might turn out to be impossible if, as is consistent with what Heidegger holds here, to engage in argument is to assume that one is a minded being whose existence is grounded in a unitary phenomenon, Being-in-the-world. For then one would have to assume that one's existence is grounded in the unitary phenomenon just to engage in argument that one's existence is grounded in the unitary phenomenon. And if one cannot escape this circularity, because there is no way of deriving the conclusion except by assuming that very conclusion in the premise-set, then (a) is indeed impossible. We cannot *show that* our Being is grounded in the unitary phenomenon, Being-in-the-world. The most we could do is show *how* our Being is so grounded. And that is precisely what Heidegger then sets out to do.

If we allow Heidegger sufficient resources to respond to our basic concern in this way, his deliverance does come at a price. It seems we must correspondingly weaken his stance towards his crucial claim, that our existence is grounded in a unitary phenomenon. He would not be *showing that* this claim is true (strong). He might not even be offering *assurance* that this claim is true (moderate). All he might be in a position to offer is effective protection against philosophical inclinations to regard this claim as false (weak).

Though this stance towards the crucial claim may indeed seem weak, it should be strong enough for Heidegger's main purposes. For if this claim is the default claim, we would have no need of any 'assurance' that philosophy might offer, let alone an argument to prove us right. Indeed, Heidegger might appeal to the route we have been outlining throughout the book to discourage any residual hankering after these things. Supposing that we *do* need such philosophical assurance is characteristic of philosophers, and it is the lure of the Trojan Horse. Falling for it would divert our inquiry into the distortions and concealments characteristic of previous philosophy.

So much then for Heidegger's analysis of what grounds our Being. We have been mainly concerned with theoretical matters and seen the implications for philosophers – like Descartes and Locke – who address the possibility of the sceptical situation. We turn now to practical matters and the implications for philosophers – like Marx and Adorno – who address the actuality of the alienation condition.

5. Possible paths to pursue

Our focus has been the section of *Being and Time* called 'Preparatory fundamental analysis of Dasein', which moves slowly and with great care towards identifying the Being of Dasein. For context, read in particular sections 12–13 on Being-in-the-world and sections 14–16 on the 'worldliness' of the world. Two of Heidegger's previous lecture-courses are particularly useful; they offer supplementary points of access to the same material, making these sections more intelligible by a process of triangulation. *Ontology – The Hermeneutics of Facticity* gives insight into Heidegger's subject-matter and the questions he raises with it. *Introduction to Phenomenological Research* helps with Heidegger's methods, aims and designs. Particularly illuminating are the second and third parts, which offer comparisons and contrasts with Descartes.

Various rival 'traditions' of interpreting *Being and Time* have sprung up, so one has to be prepared for the sound of axes being ground, but introductory books can assist if used judiciously and with constant reference back to the text. Stephen Mulhall's *Heidegger and Being and Time* (2nd ed.) is an insightful and balanced guide which has done much to overturn the previous fashion for treating the first division as containing all the essential material. *The Evolution of Modern Metaphysics* by Adrian Moore offers a careful and sympathetic description of the fundamental features of Heidegger's analysis, arguing persuasively that Heidegger must be seen as a metaphysician to his fingertips. *Martin Heidegger* by Rüdiger Safranski supplies a good deal of the contextual information necessary for gaining insight into Heidegger's development towards *Being and Time*, but it can be somewhat one-sided, so read it alongside the older *Martin Heidegger; A Political Life* by Hugo Ott. *Continental Divide* by Peter Gordon focuses on the public conversation between Heidegger and Ernst Cassirer that took place at Davos in 1929, in the wake of *Being and Time*, but it also contains considerable background material of relevance to a studied reading of Heidegger's work in the 1920s. *A Parting of the Ways: Carnap, Cassirer and Heidegger* by Michael Friedman is another helpful study which takes the Davos meeting as its crux but adds the perspective of a third participant with an opposed idea of the aims and methods of philosophy: Rudolf Carnap. The reference to non-human animals in this chapter opens up issues that have proved fruitful, both for Heidegger himself (see his lecture-course of 1929–30 *The Fundamental Concepts of Metaphysics* Part 2, chapters 3–5) and for others in their criticism of Heidegger (see in particular *Of Spirit* by Jacques Derrida and *The Open* sections 12–15 by Giorgio Agamben).

8

How we face life

Heidegger re-enters philosophy with an analysis of our everyday ways of being in the world. This enables him to find his own way of coming at issues in theoretical philosophy, issues of the sort that Descartes and Locke raise when they ask about our nature as minded beings, about how we are related to the material world, and about what we can know for certain, and how. But Heidegger's re-entry into philosophy also enables him to find his own way of coming at issues in practical philosophy, issues of the sort that Marx and Adorno raise when they ask about what we need in order to live a genuinely human existence, how we should cope with our present living conditions, how and why we mislead ourselves about what is in our best interests.

What focuses Heidegger's attention here, as we shall see, are the parallel notions of being authentic and being inauthentic. Again, we should not be daunted. It is worth recognizing that the discussion here is often more insightful than fully systematic. Heidegger says things that pull hard against each other and may well contradict each other. Exactly what it is that he proposes is thus open to widely diverging interpretation. A variety of 'existentialist' and 'Aristotelian' and 'Christian' readings have grown up in the literature. Probably there is no underlying interpretation to be found in which all of what Heidegger says on these subjects stands out as strictly coherent and consistent. Readers must make decisions about which features are of deepest structural significance to him and on that basis justify side-lining other elements.

Heidegger speaks directly to practical matters, but he never loses sight of his more theoretical task: the analysis of Dasein. Indeed, as we shall see, his approach becomes so much a blend of the practical and theoretical that the distinction largely falls away. Together with his unitary analysis of our Being as Being-in-the-world, this makes his re-entry into philosophy a deeply unifying project.

1. Being authentic

According to Heidegger, as we know,

> Dasein is an entity which in each case I myself am. Mineness belongs to any existent Dasein, and belongs to it as the condition which makes authenticity and inauthenticity possible. (53; all page references in this chapter are to Martin Heidegger's *Being and Time*; see the Bibliography for full details)

The most striking feature about this passage, certainly as one reads it in the context of *Being and Time* as a whole, is how deeply and usefully emblematic it is. Right at the start of his analysis of Dasein, Heidegger announces that he has practical issues in mind. For his concern with authenticity and inauthenticity is very directly a concern with how we live our everyday lives, how we should cope with present living conditions, how we mislead ourselves about these things. Moreover, this passage hints at the crucial connecting role he will give to authenticity and inauthenticity. They form a junction point, where more theoretical concerns with our Being directly confront more practical concerns with our living conditions. And Heidegger makes the traffic go in both directions: what he says about each such concern both determines and is determined by what he says about the other.

(i) Authenticity

It is immediately notable that Heidegger uses one specific group of words to convey authenticity and its aspects – *eigentlich; Eigenschaft; eignen; geeignet; uneigentlich; eigenst*. He could have chosen from a variety of other, more standard German terms – *authentisch; echt; Echtheit; Berechtigung*. What makes Heidegger's words a group is that they share a common stem: '*Eigen*'. This stem is the same as the English word 'own', as it occurs in phrases like 'my own self' or 'your own character'. (Not as the word occurs in 'I own this bicycle' or 'I own my house', for which German has different words.) It is with this own-ness, for Heidegger, that authenticity has essentially to do. Authenticity, for him, has essentially to do with being what is one's own.

That may seem a stilted way of putting it, of course, but this is no bad thing. The awkwardness keeps us alert to the fact that Heidegger's notion of authenticity is somewhat at variance with everyday usage. It is studiedly more formal and abstract, avoiding detail and specificity. We do need to be alert about this.

'Authentic' is a reasonably common word, and we commonly apply it to a whole variety of things: people, objects, actions, events, states of affairs. With so many uses to cover, it can be hard to give *the* meaning of the term, but we normally understand what is being said without difficulty: that the thing in question is genuine, sincere, true, not false, not fake, not corrupted, not debased. Now some of this common understanding may be playing a role in Heidegger's discussion. Certainly his commentators have tended to assume so. But a question mark hangs over this, at least if we stick to the evidence and steer clear of sheer guesswork.

We should certainly not saddle Heidegger with views he tries consciously to avoid. Our awareness of his theoretical enterprise stands us in good stead here. It should put us on guard against paraphrases that have Heidegger saying authenticity is a matter of 'being one's own self', being 'in accord with one's self', being 'in harmony with one's self', 'being true to one's self' and the like. For what is this 'self' with which one must be 'in accord'? And what is it to be 'true to' or 'in accord with' such a 'self'? As we know, Heidegger explicitly introduces quasi-specialized terms like 'Dasein' to replace such phrases and the thinking they condition, so integral to previous philosophy, so complicit with its failure to raise the question of the meaning of Being.

What concerns him is not only the theoretical baggage such phrases import but the practical baggage also. In his use, so he often insists, 'authenticity' is not an evaluative term at all. What it denotes need not be either good or desirable (167; 175–6; 179).

(ii) Own-ness

Heidegger makes different claims about authenticity in a variety of places, and we shall be interested in each. But underlying them all is the significance attributed to own-ness.

At one point, for example, Heidegger describes 'the *authentic Self* as 'the Self which has been taken hold of (*ergriffenen*) in its own way (*eigens*)' (129). Note the *Eigen*-word. At another point, he implies that, to be authentic, Dasein must 'bring itself face to face with itself' (*vor es selbst*) (184). In telling us why he thinks 'anticipation' is so significant – it enables authenticity – Heidegger also informs us about what he thinks authenticity is. Being authentic, Dasein 'discloses itself to itself', understanding its 'ownmost and uttermost' (*eigensten äusstersten*) Being (263). Note again the *Eigen*-word. In telling us why he thinks 'the voice of conscience' is so important – it enables Dasein's return from inauthenticity – Heidegger informs us about authenticity. Being authentic, Dasein 'takes hold' of its possibilities of Being, undertaking the 'burden of explicitly choosing these possibilities', keeping it definite who has 'really' (*eigentlich*) done the choosing (268). Note again the *Eigen*-word. And in telling us why he identifies 'authentic Being-one's-Self' (*eigentliches Selbstsein*) with 'resoluteness', Heidegger tells us yet more. Being authentic brings Dasein into a current, concernful and solicitous Being-with others; it does not detach Dasein from the world or isolate it as a free-floating entity (298).

The deep etymological relations that *Eigen*-words allow Heidegger to establish – between authenticity (*Eigentlichkeit*) and own (*eigen*) and ownmost (*eigenst*) – imply the kind of 'own-ness' that is present in things that belong to each other. So we may understand 'own-ness' and what is 'ownmost' in terms of what belongs to oneself. But there is need for caution. It is always tempting to think of what belongs to oneself as what is *owned* by oneself, *possessed* by oneself, something over which one *exercises* ownership or possession. Yet Heidegger explicitly resists understanding authenticity in these terms (which include particular varieties of ownership or possession like self-ownership). We can guard against the temptation to distort his view here by bearing in mind that neither 'own' nor 'belong' need take this very particular form. We talk of 'one's own family' and 'one's own town' and mean that one belongs to them, without implying either ownership or possession, in either direction – one neither owns nor is owned by them.

Is it acceptable to paraphrase 'own-ness' and what is 'ownmost' in terms of what is 'proper' and 'most proper' to us? Perhaps. Again, Heidegger is careful to be open about this. We may take what he says as inviting us to think of 'own-ness' and what is 'ownmost' as what is distinctive or individual about us. But, again, there is the need for caution. It is clear that, as Heidegger thinks of it, what is ownmost may well include features that an existent Dasein shares with others. It could be that what is distinctive about an existent Dasein is more a matter of the way its various common features are arranged than of genuinely unique features. So we should not assume that what is 'ownmost' necessarily means what is peculiar, exclusive or unique to that Dasein.

(iii) Mineness

Heidegger regards the 'own-ness' of any existent Dasein as expressed in its thinking of itself as 'mine'. And authenticity has essentially to do with being what is one's own. So he regards this 'mineness' as the condition that makes authenticity possible. This is the burden of the quoted passage.

The first-personal form of his claim – 'Dasein is an entity which in each case *I myself am*' – needs stressing. Heidegger might simply have said 'The Being of this entity is *its own*' or 'the kind of Being which belongs to Dasein is of a sort which any of us may call his own'. But he consistently chooses to express the own-ness of Dasein in terms of its 'mineness'. Elsewhere, for example, he says of Dasein that 'the Being of any such entity is in each case *mine*' (42).

What is the reason for this? It is not just that the name of the feature, 'mineness', acts as a constant reminder of its character. Heidegger also seems to be drawing attention to an implication of his method. To adopt phenomenology, recall, is to 'let that which shows itself be seen from itself'. And what Heidegger is saying is that the individuals in question here are such that they think and express their Being in the first person. Indeed, his point seems to be that it is only from this first-personal perspective that what is ownmost about Dasein shows itself from itself. That is why there is something essentially and irreducibly first-personal about Dasein. And it is why Heidegger insists on speaking always of the own-ness of Dasein in terms of its 'mineness'.

To emphasize this, we shall from now on and wherever possible convert the relevant third-personal terms into their first-personal form. Thus we will say of Heidegger's notion of authenticity that it has essentially to do with being what is my own, what is ownmost to myself.

But we should not distort the point in giving it this emphasis. Heidegger is not claiming that *all* there is to Being is that Being which is mine. He is no solipsist. He is perfectly accommodating of the fact that there are other individuals in the world. Indeed, his view – as we now know – is that authenticity necessarily brings Dasein into solicitous Being-with others. His point is just that, being Dasein (whether authentic or inauthentic), each of these individuals must be able to say of themselves 'the Being of *this* entity is *mine*'.

(iv) Practical significance

Being authentic ought to matter practically to us, to the way we organize and live our lives. So it is reasonable to think that the analysis on which authenticity depends – the analysis of Dasein – must have practical significance for us.

There are other reasons to think so. One is more oblique. However much being authentic ought to matter to us, it does not usually impinge on the way we live our ordinary, everyday lives. This may seem paradoxical, but it is not. It matters, after all, if what ought to matter to us does not usually matter to us. And because this matters, in a practical way, the analysis on which authenticity depends also has practical significance for us.

Another reason goes deeper in this direction. Heidegger is vividly aware that our interest in being authentic is sporadic at best and more theoretical and reflective than practical and engaged. His explanation is that we have a deep tendency to being inauthentic, failing in regard to what is one's own. As we shall see, he makes use of a number of subtle probes and illustrations to argue that this inauthenticity manifests itself everywhere, in almost every way we face life – or, more aptly, fail to face life. And because inauthenticity has this deep practical significance for us, so must the analysis on which it depends.

2. Being inauthentic: General framework

Heidegger goes into far more detail about inauthenticity – my failing in regard to what is my own – than about authenticity. This presents us with an opportunity: to use what we discover about inauthenticity to help clarify what he means by its converse. But we should be careful not to focus all our attention here. Inauthenticity is, after all, a sort of failure. And we can only learn so much about what it is to succeed at something by focusing on what it is to fail at it. There is a risk of ending up with distorted notions otherwise.

(i) Inauthenticity

Heidegger identifies Dasein's tendency towards being inauthentic with a term that is usually translated as 'falling' (*Verfallen*). This may sound as if Heidegger were saying that Dasein has dropped down from some higher form or grade of existence. But he denies this, and even adds: 'This term [falling] does not express any negative evaluation' (175).

Indeed, he emphatically denies that Dasein's being fallen means that it exists in a bad or deplorable state, let alone a state from which it might one day advance 'higher'.

Heidegger also describes Dasein's being inauthentic as a state of 'groundless floating'. This may sound as if he were saying that, in being inauthentic, Dasein's existence is no longer grounded in the unitary phenomenon, Being-in-the-world. But again, he firmly denies that this is so. Indeed, he insists that what makes it possible for Dasein to be inauthentic is precisely that it remains Being-in-the-world, something for which Being remains an issue:

> Dasein *can* fall only *because* Being-in-the-world, understandingly with a state of mind, is an issue for it. (179)

An analogy may help us make sense of what Heidegger seems to be saying here. Over-familiarity with the scene before us does not actually *hide* whatever we describe as 'hiding in plain sight', but it prevents us from noticing it, so we overlook it. In the same way, when I enter into the 'groundless floating' of being inauthentic, I may fail to notice even what is ownmost about myself, even though my existence does not stop being grounded in Being-in-the-world and even though I do not drop down to a lower status of existence.

This overlooking can take extreme forms. For example, I may overlook the fact that my Being is grounded in the unitary phenomenon Being-in-the-world. I may even fail to notice a crucial aspect of what is ownmost to any existent Dasein: that Being is an issue for me.

(i) The they

How might I fall into inauthenticity and thus fail to notice what is ownmost about myself? Heidegger's answer starts out from a familiar observation. In everyday living, I have a tendency to think what I think 'because one thinks such things', to say what I say 'because one says such things', to do what I do 'because that is what one does'. In other words, I tend to lose myself in a group, to become absorbed into a collectivity. Heidegger's German word for this collectivity (*das Man*) is often translated as 'the they', though it is formed from the word that we would translate into English as 'one', as in 'one thinks things', 'one says such things' and 'that is what one does'.

> This downward plunge into and within the groundlessness of the inauthentic Being of the they has a kind of motion which constantly tears the understanding away from the projecting of authentic possibilities. (178)

This 'downward plunge' and 'motion' has four features that interest Heidegger. These are the characteristic ways in which losing myself in the they presents itself to me. Most obviously, it presents itself as *tempting*. There is something both safe and reassuring, if not also appealing and attractive, about thinking what others think, saying what they say, doing what they do.

Carrying on in this way is also and inevitably *tranquillizing*, which may also be an attraction. Relying on the group, I do not have to stimulate myself about what to think or say or do while carrying on busily enough with the appearance of thinking and saying and doing things.

Allowing myself to become absorbed into the they is also *entangling*. For Heidegger insists that talk of 'losing myself' has to be taken at face value here. When I allow myself to become absorbed into the they, I overlook my own individuality and disregard what is ownmost about myself.

And this, finally, is *alienating*. For in losing myself in the they, I fail in regard to what is my own, what is proper to myself becomes confused with what is not, and thus I risk becoming divided against myself. Heidegger is careful to distinguish what he means here:

> this alienation cannot mean that Dasein gets factically torn away from itself. On the contrary, this alienation drives it into a kind of Being which borders on the most exaggerated 'self-dissection'. (178)

(ii) Occasions of inauthenticity

Heidegger is interested also in the kinds of occasion in which I lose myself in the they. He picks out three for closer examination.

The first he calls 'Idle talk'. When I say what I say because 'one' says such things, my attention concentrates not on the subject of the conversation but on what is being said about it. This talk 'idles' because there is no real attempt to get at a subject, no genuine focus of attention:

> 'Idle talk' is constituted by just such gossiping and passing the word along – a process by which its initial lack of grounds to stand on becomes aggravated to complete groundlessness. And indeed this idle talk is not confined to vocal gossip, but even spreads to what we write, where it takes the form of 'scribbling'. (168–9)

Heidegger contrasts 'idle talk' with what he calls 'discourse'. In 'discourse', I remain focused on what is being spoken about, not submerging this interest beneath my concerns about whatever is being said.

A second kind of occasion in which I lose myself in the they Heidegger calls 'curiosity'. When I say what I say because 'one' says such things, I am vulnerable to being caught up in whatever is 'new', just because it *is* new. My attention thus dissipates, Heidegger thinks, tending towards mere curiosity in the alien and the exotic:

> it does not seek the leisure of tarrying observantly, but rather seeks restlessness and the excitement of continual novelty and changing encounters. (172)

Heidegger contrasts 'curiosity' with what he calls 'attunement', where I remain properly focused on what is genuinely of interest.

A third kind of occasion in which I lose myself Heidegger calls 'ambiguity'. When I say what I say because 'one' says such things, there is no guarantee that I mean the same thing by what I say. Knowing what others mean then becomes difficult or impossible, putting the opportunity for mutual understanding and genuine communication at risk:

> Thus Dasein's understanding in the they is constantly going wrong in its projects, as regards the genuine possibilities of Being. Dasein is always ambiguously 'there' – that is to say, in that public disclosedness of Being-with-another where the loudest idle talk and the most

ingenious curiosity keep 'things moving', where, in an everyday manner, everything (and at bottom nothing) is happening. (174)

Heidegger contrasts 'ambiguity' with what he calls 'understanding'. Here, the exchange in which I take part remains committed to mutual understanding and genuine communication.

(iii) Inauthenticity about authenticity

When we first set about trying to understand Heidegger on the subject of authenticity, in the previous chapter and at the start of this, we described his position in the following way: authenticity has essentially to do with being what is one's own, what is ownmost about oneself, and glossed this in terms of what is proper to, peculiar to or belongs to oneself.

We are now in a position to appreciate two related points about this description. First, though it is not false, it does not bring out the first-personal aspect, which Heidegger regards as essential. The own-ness of Dasein is to be thought of in terms of its 'mineness'. Second, though this description in terms of 'one' and 'oneself' is not necessarily an inauthentic way of describing authenticity, it is precisely the way in which I *would* put things if I *were* being inauthentic, falling in with the they – fending off what authenticity requires of *me* by framing it in terms of what it requires of *one*, of *the they*.

These points are related. I might well realize and sustain my tendency towards being inauthentic by choosing a form of words that covers over and conceals what authenticity requires: that *I* be essentially concerned with what is *my own*, what is ownmost about *myself*. To engage in the 'one' and 'oneself' subterfuge would manifest 'ambiguity' because it would (usefully) never be clear – even to myself perhaps – whether I was speaking of myself or not, whether I was including myself in this group. And if I use such talk to avoid directing my words at myself or to dissipate my attention over an amorphous assemblage, this would also manifest 'idle talk' and 'curiosity' respectively. Such talk would be 'tempting' because it would be reassuringly indirect, 'tranquillizing' because it would excuse me from action, 'entangling' because it would overlook what is ownmost about myself and 'alienating' because it would risk confusing me with what is not me.

Conversely, my best chance of escaping these enthralments would be to keep the essential first-personal aspect of authenticity always in focus. To think and speak of authenticity as essentially to do with being what is *my own* would not only help preserve my thought and talk as 'discourse' (because that would help keep the focus on the subject-matter – in this case, myself), but it would help keep my thought and talk 'attuned' (because this subject-matter would be what is relevant and genuinely of interest to the issue – in this case, authenticity) and it would also help preserve my thought and talk as 'understanding' (because it would help keep what I mean clear enough to sustain genuine communication).

(iv) Pessimism

Heidegger evidently thinks that inauthenticity is a deep feature of Dasein. Indeed, on several occasions he implies that nothing is deeper. For example, in a passage where he characterizes the inauthenticity of Dasein in terms of its failure to 'bring itself face to face with itself', he goes on to say

> It turns away from itself in accordance with its ownmost inertia of falling (*eigensten Zug des Verfallens*). (184)

This phrase, 'its ownmost inertia of falling', is very striking. On a natural reading, it means that inauthenticity – denoted by 'falling' and depicted here as a kind of 'inertia' – is among what is 'ownmost' (*eigenst*) to Dasein.

This expresses a very strong pessimism, of course. It means not only that Dasein is *liable* to being inauthentic but that being inauthentic belongs to Dasein as one of the features that is most proper to it, most peculiar to it – like being situated, being related understandingly towards

Being, having 'mineness' and being grounded in Being-in-the-world. If Heidegger thinks inauthenticity goes *this* deep, we would expect him to treat the 'falling' which denotes it as part of his fundamental analysis, his 'analytic of Dasein'.

And this is precisely what Heidegger does do. At one point, for example, he asserts that 'falling reveals an essential ontological structure of Dasein itself' (179). And at another, he claims that 'falling is a definite existential characteristic of Dasein itself' (176). Indeed, he emphatically denies that falling is one of Dasein's more superficial properties, which he terms 'ontic', in contrast with what is 'ontological' (179). And he turns mildly metaphorical to drive the point home: we should not think of falling as the 'night view' of Dasein, its 'nocturnal side'; instead, we should recognize that falling 'constitutes all Dasein's days in their everydayness' (179; in setting up the contrast, Heidegger seems to have something like Mr Hyde's relationship with Dr Jekyll in mind).

To treat inauthenticity as among what is ownmost to Dasein has fascinating implications, of course. But this pessimism also raises deep worries. We shall be returning regularly to explore this theme in this chapter and the next.

3. Being inauthentic: Particular instances

So far we have been looking at the general framework of Heidegger's account of inauthenticity. He likes to give an impression of order and systematicity. But his descriptions of particular instances tend to bulge beyond the overall pattern. And often, what is most interesting crops up in the details of his analysis. So we shall look more closely at what he says about one particular characteristic, 'tranquillization', and one type of episode, 'curiosity'.

(i) Tranquillization

Self-assurance and decidedness often come with absorption in the they, according to Heidegger. Such everyday inauthenticity brings with it the confidence that all is in the best order, the conviction that all the possibilities worth having are open to 'one', the sense that 'one' is already living a full and significant life. Heidegger thinks these effects explain a prevalent feature of everyday living: that I assume there is really no need to seek for authentic understanding. For if what is required to be myself is already known and available to me, what would be the point? This is what lies at the heart of 'tranquillization'. And Heidegger is well aware that there is a paradoxical quality to this characteristic:

> This tranquillization in inauthentic being does not seduce one into stagnation and inactivity, but drives one to uninhibited 'hustle'. Being-fallen into the world does not now somehow come to rest. The tempting tranquillization aggravates the falling. (177–8)

In some senses of the word 'tranquil', everyday inauthenticity certainly counts as such. There is (presumably) something soothing, relaxing, calming about the thought that 'one' is already leading a full and significant life. But in other senses of the word – 'serene', 'still', 'quiet' – everyday inauthenticity is certainly not tranquil. Rather the opposite, according to Heidegger, who identifies an unexpected 'uninhibited hustle' to the tranquillization in inauthentic being.

(ii) Curiosity

It is receptivity to phenomena which makes us aware of this 'uninhibited hustle' at the heart of everyday inauthenticity. Heidegger's phenomenological method now requires him to analyse it. He chooses to do so by appeal to a specific sort of case:

> With special regard to the interpretation of Dasein, the opinion may now arise that understanding the most alien cultures and 'synthesizing' them with one's own may lead to Dasein's becoming, for the first time thoroughly and genuinely enlightened about itself. Versatile curiosity and restlessly 'knowing it all' masquerade as a universal understanding of Dasein. (178)

The point is an odd one and easily mischaracterized as a side-swipe at low-quality ethnology. What Heidegger is actually getting at it is rather deeper, and the key is in the notion of a masquerade.

Recall that, in Heidegger's view, the attempt to re-direct philosophy into the route of a perfectly sound inquiry requires raising the question of the meaning of Being. Dasein is regarded as particularly suited to this because it is related understandingly towards its own Being. This is the basis for Heidegger's optimistic audacity about the phenomenological method: that Dasein is in intimate relation with philosophy, as it is properly to be conceived. It is the essential task of philosophy to face the very issue to which Dasein is understandingly related, the question of the meaning of Being. So philosophy ought to make Dasein its point of access, designing its inquiry around what shows itself in Dasein, letting it be seen from Dasein.

Return now to Heidegger's thought that the 'hustle' of absorption in the they leads to an interest in alien or foreign cultures. His worry seems to be that I might represent myself as pursuing sound inquiry as thus conceived, raising the question of the meaning of Being in the way to which Dasein is particularly suited.

But recall also that Dasein has another essential feature: its 'mineness', which Heidegger describes as the condition that makes authenticity and inauthenticity possible. Thinking in terms of Dasein is thinking in terms of the individual which each of us can recognize as *the Dasein I am*. So that to which Dasein is particularly suited is actually inquiry into itself, the individual each of us is, not the pursuit of a *universal* understanding of Dasein. But it is precisely to such a pursuit that the 'hustle' of absorption in the they leads me. The interest in alien or foreign cultures represents itself as the attempt to identify and understand a supposed general form of being, common to all Dasein.

So I may, while engrossed in the they, represent myself as pursuing a sound inquiry, but this will be appearance only. When I take up an interest in other cultures while so engrossed, I am not raising the question of the meaning of Being in the way to which Dasein is particularly suited. That is a masquerade. What I manifest instead is only a curiosity that passes itself off as 'enlightenment' or 'understanding'. And this curiosity is the mark of the inauthentic, of failing in regard to what is my own, what is ownmost about me:

> But at bottom it remains indefinite what is really to be understood, and the question has not even been asked. Nor has it been understood that understanding itself is a potentiality-for-being which must be made free in one's ownmost Dasein alone. (178)

(iii) Alienation

The curiosity stimulated by the 'hustle' of absorption in the they is an example of inauthentic everyday modes of being. But we know this, so far, only by appeal to the essential features of Dasein. To embed the point squarely within his phenomenological method, Heidegger characterizes the 'feel' of this curiosity. It is, he claims, profoundly alienating:

> When Dasein, tranquillized, and 'understanding' everything, thus compares itself with everything, it drifts towards an alienation in which its ownmost potentiality-for-being is hidden from it. Falling Being-in-the-world is not only tempting and tranquillizing; it is at the same time alienating. (178)

Heidegger means 'alienating' in the strong sense, where I feel divided not just from others and the world but also from myself. And this division, recall, is to be thought of as 'the most exaggerated "self-dissection"'.

The explanation in this particular case seems to be that there is a cost to passing off curiosity about other cultures as an inquiry into the meaning of Being: that the focus of the genuine inquiry, what is ownmost to me as Dasein, becomes hidden. What Heidegger seems to have in mind is that I have hidden it from myself, in order to sustain the make-believe that my pretend inquiry is the real thing. This gives a distinct reason to regard the curiosity in question as inauthentic. If it is essential to Dasein to be related understandingly towards its own Being, then the attempt to hide what is ownmost to me as Dasein is a peculiarly deep way of failing in regard to what is my own.

So Heidegger is alive to the subtle ways that alienation in everyday modes of being can be palatable. Absorption in the they can even enable what passes for inquiry into the question of the meaning of Being to flourish. Through absorption in the they and the 'hustle' and curiosity it stimulates, everyday living can represent itself as *not* dividing me from others, my world, my own activity, its products and ourselves; as *not* depriving what I do of meaning; as *not* denying significance to what I am. But this all just masquerade. In Heidegger's view, it is not just that what flourishes under absorption in the they is bogus, not a genuine inquiry into the question of the meaning of Being. The real danger is that, by engaging in what merely passes for inquiry into the question of the meaning of Being, I submit to behaviour that is divisive and alienating. In particular, I hide what is ownmost to myself from myself. So while I think I am doing something unifying and significance bearing, I am in fact promoting the alienation condition, at least under Heidegger's conception of what that condition comes to.

4. Comparisons and contrasts

This return to the alienation condition recalls Adorno, inviting a comparison and contrast with Heidegger from which we stand to learn more about both.

Heidegger is evidently as committed as Adorno to the virtues of smaller-scale studies of everyday modes of living. But the styles contrast. Where Adorno offers dense portrayals, Heidegger relies on poignant observation and the occasional evocative remark. And the approaches differ, matching a deeper disparity in methods and ideals of philosophizing. For Heidegger, after all, these are studies in phenomenology, whose aim is to let what shows itself be seen from itself. Nevertheless, strong formal similarities exist. The final paragraph of the previous section would serve as a straightforward summary of the Adorno passage examined in Chapter 6, if we simply replace 'absorption in the they' with 'capitalism' and 'inquiry into the question of the meaning of Being' with 'present-giving'.

(i) Alienation

There are deeper similarities of content in their analyses of alienation. Heidegger and Adorno agree, for example, that alienation is not always *overtly* divisive, something that *flagrantly* strips our lives of meaning. Thus both pick on apparently unifying and significance-bearing activities for their representative examples: a commitment to present-giving for Adorno, an interest in the question of the meaning of Being for Heidegger. They also agree that, despite such appearances, such alienation *is* divisive; it *does* threaten to strip our lives of meaning. Thus both use their smaller-scale studies of the everyday to highlight ways in which our activities tend to be a masquerade. What passes for an interest in the question of the meaning of Being, for example, is often not a genuine interest, any more than what passes for present-giving is genuine present-giving. Third, Heidegger and Adorno agree that such alienation is deep and subtle. It makes us complicit with the forces that divide us from ourselves and from the world. So one of the most telling effects, which they both note, is that we tend to co-opt ourselves into the very structures that alienate us. And finally, they both agree that no purely external remedy will suffice. The only true remedy for alienation is the one that will free us from the constraints that we impose on ourselves.

(ii) Inauthenticity

These similarities between Adorno and Heidegger are telling, but so are the differences. They differ, for example, in what they identify as the fundamental problem or harm. Adorno, like Marx before him, treats alienation as a primary phenomenon, one of the fundamental harms that explain why capitalism certainly ought to be overthrown, and perhaps will be. Heidegger on the other hand treats alienation as a secondary phenomenon. It is the upshot of a more fundamental harm, which he identifies with the tendency towards inauthenticity, failing in regard to what is my own. This is the most general and fundamental explanation for what is problematic in our condition.

Being alienated on Heidegger's account is just one of several characteristic ways in which living an inauthentic life manifests itself as such. It takes its place alongside temptation, tranquillization and entanglement. Hence it is inauthenticity we must analyse, if we are to get to the roots of our condition. To focus on alienation instead, as if that were our fundamental malaise, might itself be alienating. For in treating what is a secondary effect as the primary cause, it would be side-stepping our true condition, and thus doing what is inauthentic and alienating.

(iii) Resolution

Given that Heidegger differs from Adorno about the real harm in our condition, it is not surprising that he differs also about its remedy. This marks an even deeper contrast between them. For Heidegger, the harms associated with inauthenticity are general, not reserved to the times and places where any particular economic system holds sway (e.g. capitalism). So it will not be sufficient to substitute our present economic system for another (e.g. communism). Indeed, to pursue that option would again evade the deep truth about our condition. So it would be inauthentic and might drive us yet further into the alienation condition. To resolve matters, we must do so at a much more fundamental level: by addressing our tendency towards inauthenticity. Thus Heidegger's resolution must be markedly different from that proposed by Marx and Adorno.

But what is the resolution that Heidegger offers? This is a difficult but vitally important issue. The short answer is that it is not obvious that Heidegger *does* offer a resolution. Much depends, as we shall see, on whether he thinks it is even possible for us to live in a fully and genuinely authentic way, which is itself difficult to determine. Certainly he gives us no reason to suppose that a remedy for inauthenticity or the condition of alienation it brings with it might be found through adoption of another system. For him, they seem to be the kind of deep harms that survive the replacement of one system by another.

5. Questions: General analysis

(i) Positive features

Is Heidegger's account of the alienation condition an improvement on Marx and Adorno? There are a number of reasons that may encourage us to think so.

First, it seems more balanced, because it places alienation alongside other features (temptation; tranquillization; entanglement). Then it seems structurally richer, because it separates positive from negative manifestations and then makes distinctions in each group (discourse versus idle talk, attunement versus curiosity, understanding versus ambiguity). Third, it seems more even-handed, because it treats alienation as one among several manifestations of a deeper phenomenon, inauthenticity. Fourth, it seems more widely acceptable, because the harm it identifies is not reserved to any particular time or place, so the responsibility for it does not rest with any economic system or class. If the responsibility lies anywhere, it lies with each existent Dasein, so capable of hiding that which is most itself from itself. Finally, it seems more plausible, because it is cautious about the possibility of a resolution.

On the other hand, Heidegger's account of alienation rests on his analysis of authenticity and inauthenticity. And significant questions arise about this analysis.

(ii) Questionable features

Heidegger's analysis of authenticity, in terms of what is ownmost to me, seems rather schematic. It is a formal and abstract analysis, precise enough perhaps, but neither detailed nor very specific. We have acknowledged this from the start. Is this a problem for Heidegger?

Many think it is. Indeed, some treat it as a major fault, one of the fundamental reasons to reject Heidegger's whole enterprise in *Being and Time*. At the heart of this critique lie two claims. One is that Heidegger's analysis of authenticity is indeed as schematic as it seems. The other is that Heidegger assigns a role to this analysis – being readily applicable to the concrete situations in which we live our lives, a measure by which we can tell in particular cases whether a person is acting authentically or not – which requires that the analysis be both detailed and specific.

If these two claims hold, there is little difficulty in showing that a major fault must indeed lie at the heart of Heidegger's project. Being schematic, his analysis of authenticity must fail to be detailed and specific. If matched with particular cases and pressed into acting as their measure, it could only ever produce vague, ambiguous and equivocating statements.

(iii) Is the analysis mere 'jargon'?

We find this line of criticism, for example, in Adorno. Adorno offers a host of critical reflections on Heidegger, but it is the exuberant critique of his views on authenticity in *The Jargon of Authenticity* that is best known and most powerful. This book now exists as a separate work, but it was designed to be integrated into the full-length critique of Heidegger included in *Negative Dialectics*. *The Jargon of Authenticity* is regularly and brutally unfair to Heidegger, shedding at least as much light on its author as on its target. But it does work as an effective antidote to that tendency towards uncritical prostration which Heidegger's work on existential themes can sometimes induce.

Adorno condemns Heidegger for reducing 'authenticity' to a mere jargon word, something that purports to be detailed and specific but which is actually as vacuous and ambiguous as the ideas it covers for. Indeed, Adorno accuses Heidegger of a deeper design: of making 'authenticity' vacuous and ambiguous on purpose, so that the compliant reader will fill the free-floating term with 'the pretence of deep human emotion', thus giving it a cultic resonance that is 'noble and homey at once' and making it peculiarly apt to voice 'the dark drives of the intelligentsia before 1933' (*The Jargon of Authenticity* pp. 2–3).

But we might question the two claims that lie at the heart of this 'jargon' accusation. Consider the first. Is Heidegger's analysis of authenticity really as schematic as it appears? Many sympathetic commentators think not. They claim to find evidence of a detailed and specific account in *Being and Time*, one that goes far beyond the schematic analysis in terms of what is ownmost to me.

Considerable ingenuity and creativeness have gone into supporting this strategy. This is unsurprising, since what Heidegger does say on the subject is so dispersed and unsystematic. It requires much energy to extrapolate towards the detailed and specific account he is said to hold. The result is a quite bewildering array of mutually contradictory accounts, all ascribed to Heidegger: that authenticity is a matter of (i) acknowledging one's life as ultimately contingent, or (ii) denying that anything one has previously accepted as serious matters at all, or (iii) renouncing the hope that pursuing any project will give one's life meaning, or (iv) freeing oneself from conformity and illusion, or (v) being sufficiently resolute to experience one's life as freed from subjection to norms, or (vi) taking responsibility for one's participation in the normative sphere, or (vii) being true to one's self, or of being able to identify with the life one leads.

This lists only the best-known readings. If one stands back, sticks to the evidence and steers clear of sheer guesswork, it seems clear that the first claim is true. What Heidegger says about authenticity is indeed schematic, so much so that commentators feel unconstrained in ascribing him this vast range of detailed and specific positions. Any of (i)–(vii) are consistent with what he says, which is as much as to say that none are what he would clearly and demonstrably have subscribed to.

If the first claim is true, consider the second. Does Heidegger indeed assign a role to his analysis of authenticity that requires it to be detailed and specific, applicable to particular cases, a measure by which to tell whether a person is acting authentically or not on definite occasions?

It seems equally clear that this claim is false. Recall the context in which Heidegger discusses 'the condition which makes authenticity and inauthenticity possible' (53). He is inquiring into the 'basic state' of Dasein. His investigation is that of a radical, concerned at depth with what is fundamental. Hence his is a maximally general inquiry. As he continually reminds us, his task is to 'work out' the basic existential features of Dasein so that we can then – at some constantly deferred point – grasp the problem that definite ways of Being present us with (56). And authenticity is explicitly in scope here; it belongs as a fundamental and essential element of this maximally general inquiry. So we should not be surprised that it is treated like other such fundamental elements, schematically and without detail or specificity.

In short, we should take Heidegger at his word. What is schematic in his account is intended and justifiable. So we can dispense with the 'jargon' charge, and with it the urge to ascribe Heidegger a detailed and specific account of authenticity.

6. Questions: Particular instances

Let us move on to Heidegger's smaller-scale observations: Heidegger on 'understanding the most alien cultures', where what comes to the fore is one particular characteristic of alienation, 'tranquillization', and one particular type of episode, 'curiosity'. Do his observations here support his overall position?

(i) Does curiosity manifest 'hustle'?

It is worth asking whether Heidegger is right to claim that curiosity necessarily manifests the 'hustle' of tranquillization. He identifies an interest in 'the most alien cultures' with the attempt to discover a purely notional, generalized form of human existence, and he criticizes any such attempt as a manifestation of the 'hustle' of tranquillization, as inauthentic. But this line of thought may seem both unpersuasive and odd.

It may seem unpersuasive, because there is no reason to think that an interest in other cultures *must* take this purely notional form (though of course it might do). And it may seem odd, because what stimulates such an interest in other cultures might well be the contrary thought: that it is useful and perhaps even necessary to remind ourselves constantly of what is 'most alien' if we are to withstand the temptation to look for a purely notional, generalized form of existence. This contrary thought coheres nicely, of course, with Heidegger's own conception of a sound inquiry into the question of the meaning of Being.

(ii) Is curiosity necessarily alienating?

We may also question Heidegger's claim that curiosity is necessarily alienating. Given that it is possible to be 'curious' about other cultures without necessarily manifesting the 'hustle' of tranquillization – indeed, given that our curiosity may be stimulated by Heidegger's own conception of a sound inquiry into the question of the meaning of Being – it does not appear that curiosity is necessarily inauthentic, let alone necessarily alienating. I need not hide my ownmost Dasein to be interested in 'the most alien cultures'. Such an interest may be, in part, a way of evoking what is particular about and peculiar to myself.

(iii) Do we tend to be tranquillized?

Finally, we may raise a broader issue: whether Heidegger is right to claim that we tend to be involved in the 'hustle' of tranquillization. His discussion moves fast over the relevant points, so it is worth slowing him down to question the transitions he makes.

Suppose I do have a tendency to think and say and do things that whole groups think and say and do. We may nevertheless doubt whether I necessarily do so *because* any whole group thinks and says and does this. We may also doubt whether the relevant group is to be conceived as some vast single and undifferentiated entity, 'the they'. There may be many groups that exercise the relevant sort of authority over me, and I may choose between them. Indeed, I may choose to be guided by one group precisely because I identify with its rejection of the stand taken by another group.

For example, suppose the reason why I think we ought to commute by bicycle is that it is the kind of view actively promoted by *The Sunday Guardian*, and I am inclined to take on such views as my own because I identify with its rejection of the kinds of view propagated by *The Weekly Mail*. I am here identifying with a group and yet continuing to exercise my capacity to choose, to decide for myself. 'Should I identify with this group rather than that? Should I identify in these ways but not those? Should I identify at this level or strength rather than that level or strength?' And so on. Exercising choice in these ways may – one might have thought – protect me from 'losing myself' or becoming 'absorbed' into one single amorphous collectivity, 'the they'.

Now there is much Heidegger could say in response. And it is unclear anyway how much damage such particular criticisms do. For Heidegger himself subjects his smaller-scale observations to change and revision as he works through *Being and Time*. But there is a deeper kind of objection that springs from the essential features of his position, and it is to this we shall now turn.

7. Trojan Horse syndrome

It may be that the essential features of Heidegger's position entail claims that contradict each other, indeed that they lead to a series of such paradoxes. Paradoxes are a real problem, of course. They present very powerful reasons to reject a philosopher's position. For if the position leads to conclusions that contradict each other, it rules itself out of court, without the need to consider the merits of alternative positions.

We shall first identify the root issue, then describe some paradoxes that it engenders and finally look at the implications for Heidegger's overall project.

(i) Root issue

The problem arises from the combination of two basic claims we have seen Heidegger make. One concerns authenticity: that being authentic is essentially a matter of being what is ownmost to me (what belongs to me as most proper to me, most peculiar to me). The other claim concerns inauthenticity: that being inauthentic is among what is ownmost to Dasein – or to put this in the requisite first-personal terms, what is ownmost to me, as Dasein.

It seems to follow that, being Dasein, I am both inauthentic and authentic, at the same time and in the deepest sense. I am inauthentic in the deepest sense because being inauthentic is among what is ownmost to me, as Dasein. And I am at the same time authentic in the deepest sense because, in being inauthentic, I am being what is ownmost to me. And that is a contradiction. For if it is true that I am authentic in the deepest sense, it must be false that I am inauthentic in that same deepest sense, and vice versa.

This is the root issue, and it is a tangled one. Failing to be what is ownmost to me is itself what is ownmost to me. What sense can be made of this? Or indeed what sense can be made of another apparent implication of Heidegger's notion of authenticity and his sense of our deep inauthenticity: that it is authentic for me to be inauthentic and inauthentic for me to be authentic?

(ii) Paradox of being

To clarify the paradox here, it will be helpful to label the various premises and proceed more slowly.

Suppose we accept Heidegger's position, that (1) being authentic is essentially a matter of being what is ownmost to me and (2) being inauthentic is among what is ownmost to me, as Dasein. And suppose we accept what seems obvious, that (3) it cannot be that I am being both authentic and inauthentic at the same time and in the same deepest sense.

Now imagine that (4) I am being authentic in the deepest sense at time T. From (1), (3) and (4), it follows that (5) I cannot be being inauthentic in the deepest sense at T. That is one conclusion that is of interest to us.

Consider now a second argument. From (1) and (4), it follows that (6) I am being what is ownmost to me at T. And from (2) to (6), it follows that (7) I am being inauthentic in the deepest sense at T. That is the second conclusion of interest to us.

These two conclusions, (5) and (7), obviously contradict each other. And we derive them using valid argument-forms from Heidegger's analysis, together with a claim (3), which seems obvious. So it seems we have a genuine paradox. Without considering the merits of alternative positions on these matters, this alone may give us good reason to question and perhaps reject Heidegger's analysis.

(iii) Paradox of philosophy

More paradoxes appear once we add further elements of Heidegger's position. One is of particular interest since it binds together central themes from the present chapter with the previous chapter. We will express the issue in the first person, in accord with the current directive.

Recall the reasons Heidegger has for audacious optimism. (1) The proper task of philosophy is to raise the question of the meaning of Being, (2) we require the phenomenological method to perform this task, which is 'to let that which shows itself be seen from itself in the very way in which it shows itself from itself', and (3) as Dasein, I am such that Being is always and already in question for me. Heidegger takes (1)–(3) to show that (4) as Dasein, I am an appropriate point of access for philosophy. This is a concise way of saying that to design philosophical inquiry around what shows itself in me, letting it be seen from me, in the way it shows itself from me, is to re-enter philosophy in a way that does what is proper and essential for philosophy.

But now consider Heidegger's claim that (5) being inauthentic is among what is ownmost to me, as Dasein. On his own understanding, (6) to be inauthentic is for me to fail to bring myself 'face to face' with myself, to 'turn away' from myself in accordance with my 'ownmost inertia of falling'. From (5 to (6) and (1) to(2), it surely follows that (7) as Dasein, I *cannot* be an appropriate point of access for philosophy. For being inauthentic at the deepest level (5), I must be turned away from whatever shows itself in me, unable to see it in the very way it shows itself from me (6). So I cannot be the appropriate point of access for the phenomenological method (2), the method which is necessary to perform the proper task of philosophy (1). Indeed, were I to make myself the point of access, I would fail to raise the question of the meaning of Being.

So again we have two conclusions, (4) and (7), which straightforwardly contradict each other. And the upshot this time is more troubling still. For Heidegger seems to be undermining his own most fundamental efforts.

The problem is this. As we know, Heidegger's fundamental aim is to re-enter philosophy, superseding previous efforts by raising the question of the meaning of Being. And in trying to accomplish this, he draws into the heart of his position a commitment to two claims. One reflects his audacious optimism: as Dasein, we are an appropriate point of access for philosophy. The other reflects his deep pessimism: that our inauthenticity is ownmost to us as Dasein. The combination, as we have just discovered, entails that our philosophizing must fail to raise the question of the meaning of Being.

So we fall back into the characteristic failure of previous philosophizing. Descartes, Locke, Marx and Adorno also draw into the heart of their position a set of commitments that undermine their own most fundamental efforts. Like other philosophers, Heidegger falls for the Trojan Horse. But the failure is more poignant in his case. For he sets out in full awareness that previous philosophy tends to be systematically self-undermining. Indeed, it is precisely in trying to supersede the failed efforts of his predecessors that he finds himself in this predicament. Thus he embeds himself more firmly in their failure.

8. Practical and theoretical

Heidegger might escape this predicament if he were to renounce his pessimism. But he seems strongly committed to the view that inauthenticity is among what is ownmost to Dasein. This raises another general issue. Heidegger is strikingly optimistic and audacious in his analysis of Dasein. Bringing this out was very much the aim of the previous chapter. But Heidegger's optimism seems to dissolve when he comes to authenticity and inauthenticity. Indeed, it is the depth of his pessimism here that is striking.

We may wonder whether there is evidence here of an underlying inconsistency of outlook. For Heidegger's pessimism springs from his analysis of inauthenticity and our tendency towards it. But much that may be regarded as optimistic, at least for philosophy, springs from the same analysis. Appreciating this will enable us to round off the present discussion, before tackling Heidegger's approach to death, which returns us better equipped to judge whether he does indeed fall for the systematically self-undermining tendency characteristic of the Trojan Horse.

(i) Bridge

An example of the optimism that arises from Heidegger's analysis of inauthenticity is the bridge it allows him to build between practical and theoretical issues. We have seen something of how this works. Facing one way, towards the practical, Heidegger is able to account for the alienation condition by appeal to authenticity and inauthenticity, treating the latter as the fundamental explanation for alienation. Facing the other way, towards the theoretical, he is able to account for authenticity and inauthenticity by appeal to his analysis of Dasein and the unitary phenomenon Being-in-the-world. The particular issue here is what it is to be Dasein, to be related understandingly towards itself, to have 'mineness', to be grounded in the unitary phenomenon, Being-in-the-world. This bridge between practical and theoretical issues gives cause for optimism about our re-entry into philosophy, for each is then able to offer considerable aid to the other.

(ii) Previous philosophizing

Heidegger's diagnosis of what has gone wrong in previous philosophizing offers an immediate example. On his view, previous philosophers tend to conceive each of us as a composite of separate elements, radically divided from the world and from ourselves. This is the source of the sceptical situation and the alienation condition. The problem here may seem to be purely an issue for theoretical philosophy. But a properly directed philosophy – one that genuinely raises the question of the meaning of Being and is not lost in mere curiosity – ought to explain why philosophers tend to 'skip over' the fact that our existence is grounded in Being-in-the-world. After all, if Heidegger is right, this unitary phenomenon is just that, a *phenomenon*, something that 'shows itself'. And it is precisely philosophy's task to let what shows itself be seen from itself, in the very way in which it shows itself from itself. So it seems that, despite the efforts of very serious and committed and intelligent philosophers, philosophy itself has been failing decisively at its own essential task. How do we explain this?

It is Heidegger's answer to this question that makes the issue fully practical. Doing philosophy is a way of Being-with other Dasein. In Being-with others, I am liable to lose myself in the they (because this is tempting, not just tranquillizing, alienating or entangling). To lose myself in the they will distort my philosophizing in various ways. Most significantly, it is likely to turn my genuine inquiry into curiosity, so that crucial phenomena will go unnoticed. For example, I may 'skip over' the fact that my existence is grounded in a unitary phenomenon, Being-in-the-world, and thus threaten myself with the sceptical situation. This is how an issue for theoretical philosophy turns out to be an issue for practical philosophy also: my tendency to be inauthentic, how it arises, how it may be dealt with. Indeed, the link between practical and theoretical goes deeper still. Since losing myself in the they obscures what actually shows itself, I am failing at philosophy's essential task, which is to let what shows itself be seen from itself. Hence even the fact that my 'philosophizing' is not genuine philosophy becomes a practical issue.

(iii) Ethics and metaphysics

The bridge that authenticity and inauthenticity form between practical and theoretical issues leads to a striking conclusion. We can see this if we recall three leading elements of Heidegger's position. Heidegger thinks being authentic is a matter of being what is 'ownmost' (*eigenst*) to myself. He also thinks that raising the question of the meaning of Being is part of what it is to be what is ownmost to myself. And finally he thinks that raising this question is the fundamental task for metaphysics and calls for phenomenology. We have only to add the plausible claim that I ought to be authentic – where this is a moral 'ought' – to arrive at the conclusion that I ought to be doing metaphysics, and in the phenomenological way.

This is a surprising claim, to say the least. It implies that metaphysics and phenomenology are moral or ethical demands. Indeed, it might be morally blameworthy not to do metaphysics, and not to do it in the phenomenological way. A more modest way of putting the point is still quite striking: that it is for ethical reasons that we ought to do metaphysics.

What sort of claim is this? It may look as if it were a priority claim: that ethics must be prior to metaphysics, that it is more basic in the order of justification. But this may not be the whole story. It is possible to hold simultaneously that, just as it is for ethical reasons that we ought to do metaphysics, so it is for metaphysical reasons that we ought to do ethics. And it may well be that Heidegger holds this view. He certainly seems to think that the ethical issue of what it is for me to be authentic depends on the metaphysical issue of what it is for me to be what is ownmost to myself. And it would be fitting for him to hold that ethics and metaphysics are equally basic, neither being prior to the other in the order of justification. For if the reasons why we should do metaphysics are ethical and vice versa, they must cohere at depth. And this would cohere with the deeply unified – and unifying – character of Heidegger's approach.

9. Possible paths to pursue

Heidegger's first proper discussion of our tendencies towards inauthenticity comes towards the end of Division One of *Being and Time*, the 'Preparatory Fundamental Analysis of Dasein'. To gain a proper understanding of the extract, it is necessary to read sections 35–8 closely and then study the following discussion of care (sections 39–44) with which Heidegger identifies the Being of Dasein. This is good preparation for a reading of Division Two, where authenticity and inauthenticity come to the fore in relation to various existential themes.

Heidegger's Analytic by Taylor Carman is a thorough discussion of (in)authenticity in relation to Heidegger's 'preparatory fundamental' analysis. Carman has specific scholarly purposes in mind: to demonstrate the exact extent – the magnitude and the limits – of Heidegger's dependency on Kant and Husserl. But it is his careful consideration of authenticity and its converse, here and in subsequent papers, that are innovative and of most value in the context of this chapter. The present chapter gives reasons not to follow Carman in translating *Eigentlichkeit* as 'ownedness' (p. 285) and in overlooking Heidegger's own protestations that 'authenticity' is not to be understood as an evaluative term (p. 286). *Philosophical Myths of the Fall* by Stephen Mulhall contains an imaginative reading of Heidegger on inauthenticity (chapter 2), which does much with what Heidegger stirs up by his use of the notions of 'fall' and 'falling' and 'fallenness'. Adrian Moore's account of the fundamentals of Heidegger's analysis consciously sidesteps the issues surrounding authenticity but nevertheless reveals some of the reasons why, on Heidegger's conception, ethics and metaphysics make demands on each other. Rahel Jaeggi discusses relevant points of contrast between Heidegger and Marx in her *Alienation* (chapter 2). William Blattner provides a literature survey in his essay 'Authenticity and resoluteness'. Adorno's critique of Heidegger in *The Jargon of Authenticity* remains of interest. More unjust still but riotously funny is the anti-Heidegger rant by the character Reger in Thomas Bernhard's *Old Masters* (pp. 41–8).

9

How we face death

Heidegger launches the second half of *Being and Time* with an intense investigation of our dealings with death. In so doing, he unites theoretical and practical matters, just as when thinking about life.

Many of the same themes carry over from the first half of *Being and Time*: the analysis of Dasein, the nature of authenticity, our tendency towards inauthenticity. This reminds us of what unifies the book. Both halves belong to Part One of Heidegger's overall project, and both aim at the interpretation of Dasein. But this also draws attention to differences. Time and temporal notions suddenly acquire central significance, and this changes Heidegger's approach to familiar themes. Whether the second half is meant to correct the earlier approach or merely to complement it is a matter for debate. But it is certainly true that the treatment of existential themes – death, authenticity, resoluteness – becomes significantly richer, more complex and psychologically satisfying.

Heidegger's analysis reveals various ways in which we fail to face death, even when we appear to be most engaged in doing so. But this is not just another case study of inauthenticity in our everyday modes of being. The analysis is far more disturbing than that. To suppose we are deeply inauthentic about something that matters so deeply and so much has dramatic, even alarming, consequences.

For example, it may offer further evidence that Heidegger does indeed regard inauthenticity as among what is 'ownmost' to me as Dasein, part of my essential ontological structure. As we know, this would mean that failing to be what is ownmost to me is itself what is ownmost to me. And this leads to paradox, when coupled with

Heidegger's analysis of authenticity. It may even manifest the Trojan Horse syndrome, if he draws into the heart of his position a set of commitments that undermines his own most fundamental efforts.

So the question that Heidegger's analysis of death forces us to face is one for which this whole book prepares us.

We have seen how and why previous philosophers fall for the systematically self-undermining tendency characteristic of the Trojan Horse. We have watched Heidegger identify the various commitments that bring this about. We have experienced the hard work he imposes on us to help avoid these commitments. We have re-entered philosophy with him, focusing on the analysis of Dasein and adopting the method of phenomenology. Yet Heidegger's very attempts to escape the Trojan Horse may cause him to fall for it. Is this indeed so? And where does that leave us?

1. Being-towards-death

How we deal with death – in all senses of the usefully wide-ranging verb 'deal with' – Heidegger considers under the more focused concern of what he calls our 'Being-towards-death'. He is interested in the 'everyday' aspects of this Being-towards, the way in which death ordinarily figures for us. This is not just a matter of the way we think about and experience the deaths of others. Indeed, what primarily concerns Heidegger is the way each of us faces – or fails to face – the prospect of our own death.

(i) The first person

That is not quite the way we should put it, if we want to bring ourselves closest to what Heidegger is proposing. Better to say that what primarily concerns him is the way I face – or fail to face – the prospect of my own death.

The rationale for this first-person focus lies in features we have uncovered in the previous two chapters.

First, Dasein remains at the centre of the analysis. It is in relation to Dasein that death is being considered. And as we know, Heidegger stresses that there is something essentially and irreducibly first-personal about Dasein.

Second, phenomenology remains the method. As we know, phenomenology aims to 'let that which shows itself be seen from itself'. And given what is essentially first-personal about Dasein, it is from and to the first person that what shows itself about Dasein lets itself be seen from itself.

Finally, the analysis remains a unity of the theoretical and the practical with authenticity acting as the bridge. And Dasein's authenticity is a matter of what is 'own-most', as we know, where this own-ness is to be thought of in terms of 'mineness'.

It is for these interconnected reasons that Heidegger's focus remains closely first-personal when he comes to Dasein's 'Being-towards-death'. He could not speak more plainly about this:

> by its very essence, death is in every case mine, in so far as it 'is' at all
> (240; all page references in this chapter are to Martin Heidegger *Being and Time*; see the Bibliography for full details.)

(ii) Authenticity

To face my own death is to engage in something specific and unique for Heidegger: it is to face 'the possibility of the impossibility of any existence at all' (262). But we can best appreciate what is specific about this by attending first to what is general, for we are now reasonably familiar with the overall picture and it provides a convenient point of entry.

First then, Heidegger insists that facing my own death is a matter of facing the issues raised by my own Being as Dasein. We know much of what this involves: facing the fact that my Being belongs to those we use 'who' about, that this Being is such that Being itself is always and already in question for it, that I am related understandingly to this Being, that this Being is always and already *there*, a unitary phenomenon we call 'Being-in-the-world', and that this Being is always and already mine.

Second, Heidegger re-deploys his approach to authenticity in general to identify what is particular about being authentic in facing my own death. I must engage in what he calls 'discourse', 'attunement' and 'understanding' – by contrast with what he calls 'idle talk', 'curiosity' and 'ambiguity'. The signs that I am indeed authentically engaged are that I remain focused on what is of genuine significance, and particularly on what is 'ownmost', and that I aim at mutual understanding when I attempt to communicate.

These more general elements enable us to identify what is specific to the particular instance of death. Heidegger thinks three features would be salient to me, were I to face death in an authentic way.

First, I would be struck by the fact that I have my own death to face. No one else can die my death for me. My death is not related to anyone else as the death that it is. Heidegger expresses this in saying that death is *unbezüglich*. This is normally translated as 'non-relational', and we can continue the practice, so long as we are aware that the German is not technical or metaphysically loaded as the English phrase is. What Heidegger means to express is that I recognize I am utterly alone if I do indeed face my own death. All my relations to other Dasein are 'undone', as he puts it (250).

Second, it would be clear to me that my death is not something that can be avoided or bypassed. It strikes me as a real threat, not something I can escape or elude. Heidegger expresses this in saying that death is 'not to be outstripped'. We might assume that, recognizing this, I must set about expecting my death. But recall that death is the possibility of the impossibility of any existence at all. So it is as a *possibility* that I need to face it if I am to do so authentically. Were I to adopt an attitude of *expectation* towards my death, Heidegger thinks, that death would 'get a foothold in the actual' (262). (He may be assuming, plausibly, that to expect my death would require conceiving it for myself in concrete detail, turning it into something tangible.) So Heidegger recommends adopting an attitude of anticipation instead. To anticipate my death, he thinks, enables me to retain my understanding of it as a possibility.

Third, I would recognize that not only do I have my own death to face but also there is nothing more my own than my own death. Of all things that I face in my future, there is nothing more 'mine' than this death. Heidegger expresses this in saying that death is an 'ownmost possibility' for me. Naturally, as Dasein, I share with others the fact that I will die. But what authentic Being-towards-death focuses on is *my* death, something that is most individual to me, distinctive, peculiar, exclusive, unique. Facing this authentically means to anticipate my death, as we know. And to anticipate my death is to open myself to a constant threat, which naturally and appropriately arouses anxiety. Hence Heidegger says "Being-towards-death is essentially anxiety' (266). We might assume this means fear or fright, but Heidegger carefully distinguishes anxiety from such 'accidental or random' emotions of weakness (251). For him, anxiety is a constant attitude to a constant threat, and thus something that requires resoluteness. Thus he speaks of 'the courage for anxiety in the face of death' (254). It takes no such courage or resoluteness to feel fear or other such transient emotions.

When Heidegger gathers these general and particular elements together, he draws attention to the underlying phenomenon:

> Death is a possibility-of-Being which Dasein itself has to take over in every case. With death, Dasein stands before itself in its ownmost potentiality-for-Being. This is a possibility in which the issue is nothing less than Dasein's Being-in-the-world. (250)

There are fascinating issues here. Why does Heidegger draw such particular attention to Being-in-the-world in identifying what it is that death puts at issue? We shall address this question once we have a clearer sense of his whole position on authentic Being-towards-death. So the next task is to learn from a series of contrasts.

(iii) 'One dies'

Authentic 'Being-towards-death' requires the kind of first-personal focus that expresses itself in our use of language by a preference for phrases like 'I shall die' and 'my death'. But what Heidegger finds in our actual use of language is a marked preference for third-personal forms, like 'one dies'. We can imagine the kind of commonplace statements he has in mind: 'I wonder what happens after one dies', 'I'm sure one dies happier while sleeping', and so on.

Heidegger makes much of this tendency in our use of language; he appeals to it for evidence:

> analysis of the phrase 'one dies' reveals unambiguously the kind of being which belongs to everyday Being-towards-death. (297)

He thinks our preference for this third-personal form reveals two aspects in particular. The first reflects the way we actually understand death itself. Heidegger's claim is that, when we use the phrase 'one dies', we tend to represent death in a vague way, as *some* thing, that will come from *some* where, at *some* time. This deprives us of the sense that death is a real threat:

> In such a way of talking ['*one dies*'], death is understood as an indefinite something which, above all, must duly arrive from somewhere or other, but which is proximally *not yet objectively present* for oneself, and is therefore no threat. (297)

To represent death in this way, as something that will come, is to acknowledge that there must be something it reaches or meets, something it strikes. But use of the phrase 'one dies' enables people to appear to acknowledge this menace while still deflecting any real threat to themselves. This leads naturally to the second aspect which our preference for the third-personal forms reveals: the way we actually understand what it is that dies:

> In Dasein's public way of interpreting, it is said that 'one dies', because everyone else and oneself can talk himself into saying that 'in no case is it I myself', for this 'one' is *no one*. 'Dying' is levelled off to an occurrence which reaches Dasein, to be sure, but belongs to nobody in particular. (297)

If death belongs to anyone, it belongs to the they; but the they is no one, or no one in particular, and certainly not me.

In short, there is something markedly evasive about our preference for the third-personal form which stubbornly dominates our everyday Being-towards-death (253). And Heidegger identifies this evasiveness with the temptation to lose oneself – to lose *myself* – in a group, to become absorbed into a collectivity. Adapting his own usage to express this, he says:

> The expression 'one dies' spreads abroad the opinion that what gets reached, as it were, by death, is the they. (297)

And as we know, Heidegger thinks such dealings with 'the they' represent a 'downward plunge' into the 'groundlessness' of inauthentic Being. (178)

(iv) Inauthenticity

Being inauthentic in our Being-towards-death shares many of the same characteristics as other forms of inauthenticity. It becomes clear that, to some extent, Heidegger has a general structure in mind, which he applies to the particular case of death. So, for example, he identifies such inauthenticity with the familiar three kinds of occasion on which it manifests itself: in 'idle talk', in 'curiosity' and in 'ambiguity'.

I lose myself in mere 'idle talk' about death when I change the focus, ensuring that death itself is no longer my real concern but what we tend to *say* about death. Thus I refashion death as a public event, a recurring phenomenon:

> If idle talk is always ambiguous, so is this manner of talking about death [talking of 'one dies']. Dying, which is essentially mine in such a way that no one can be my representative, is perverted into an event of public occurrence which the they encounters. In the way of talking which we have characterized, death is spoken of as a 'case' which is constantly occurring. (297)

In an authentic Being-towards-death, 'discourse' would replace 'idle talk'. As Dasein, I would be struck by the features of *my own* death, the fact that it is 'non-relational', that *my* death is not related to anyone else as the death that it is.

I lose myself in mere 'curiosity' about death when I let my attention wander and thus treat death as a mere mishap, an oddity, a novel 'case', something distant and alien that arouses inquisitiveness rather than anxiety:

> Death gets passed off as always something 'actual'; its character as a possibility gets concealed, and so are the other two items that belong to it – the fact that it is non-relational and that it is not to be outstripped. (297)

In an authentic Being-towards-death, 'attunement' would replace 'curiosity'. As Dasein, I would remain properly receptive to my *own* death: that it is my 'ownmost' possibility, that is of all possibilities, that which is most my own, that which is most proper to *me*. Genuinely treating my death as a possibility for me would require adopting an attitude of anticipation towards it.

I lose myself in 'ambiguity' about death when I talk around the subject while purporting to talk about death. There is no common focus of attention and hence no guarantee that I mean the same things by what we all then say. This undermines the possibility of mutual understanding, for all the apparent focus on what is common between us.

> By such ambiguity, Dasein puts itself in the position of losing itself in the they as regards a distinctive potentiality-for-being which belongs to Dasein's ownmost self. The they gives its approval, and aggravates the *temptation* to cover over from oneself one's ownmost Being-towards-death. (297)

In an authentic Being-towards-death, 'understanding' would replace 'ambiguity'. As Dasein, I would recognize death as it really figures for me, something that is not to be outstripped by me, and hence opening myself to it as a constant and genuine threat. Being obliged to think of it in these terms helps me remain attentive to death as it is, and thus supports the possibility of understanding and genuine communication.

The strategy Heidegger deploys here, applying the general structure to the particular case, also guides him in characterizing the inauthenticity here. Confronted by death, it is 'tempting', 'tranquillizing', 'alienating' and 'entangling' to lose myself in the they.

I am *tempted* because being with the they helps sustain the false impression that my own death is a public event, to be talked about as such. I am *tranquillized* because being with the they enables me to sustain the feeling of leading a full and genuine life while I ignore my own death. I am *alienated* because being with the they distracts me from what is proper to me, thus dividing me from myself and rendering me incapable of being directed on the very issue which is of most significance to me. And finally I am *entangled* because I am caught up in confusion about what is proper to me and what is not, what is significant and valuable to me and what is not.

2. Inauthenticity and its depths

(i) Tolstoy and Ivan Illych

The lines of thought that structure Heidegger's analysis of our everyday Being-towards-death recall a passage from Tolstoy's novella 'The Death of Ivan Illych'. The story concerns a man who makes increasingly desperate attempts to elude thoughts about his own death, before finally turning to face it. In the midst of this process, he reflects on his own previous attitudes towards death:

> The syllogism he had learnt from Kiesewetter's Logic: 'Caius is a man, men are mortal, therefore Caius is mortal', had always seemed to him correct as applied to Caius, but certainly not as applied to himself. That Caius – man in the abstract – was mortal, was perfectly correct, but he was not Caius, not an abstract man, but a creature quite separate from all others. . . . Caius really was mortal, and it was right for him to die; but for me, little Vanya, Ivan Illych, with all my thoughts and emotions, it's altogether a different matter. It cannot be that I ought to die. That

would be too terrible. ('The Death of Ivan Illych' p. 259. Incidentally,
J. G. Kiesewetter was Kant's pupil and Clausewitz's teacher.)

These attitudes may seem strikingly close to those that Heidegger
identifies as characteristic of our everyday Being-towards-death. But
there are differences also: he evidently thinks we are more cunning and
resourceful in our inauthenticity than even Tolstoy perceives.

To think and speak in terms of 'one' ('one dies'; 'one is mortal') is
less remote than thinking and speaking in terms of 'Caius – man in
the abstract' ('Caius dies'; 'Caius is mortal'). In this use of 'one', I refer
directly to the group of which I am a member (no matter how much
I may then try to ignore or overlook the implications). But in the use
of 'Caius', I can hold off reference to myself by neglecting to perform
the inference required. This is one way in which Heidegger thinks us
more astute, more cunning, in our everyday Being-towards-death.
For in talking in terms of 'one' I can *say*, even to myself (*especially* to
myself, perhaps), that I am thereby recognizing the relevance of the
information to myself. My verbal facility is the more cunning for being
less obviously fabricated, less likely to give the game away. Confronted
by the reflections of Tolstoy's character, for example, I need not be
caused to question my own attitudes; I can respond: 'How very self-
deceiving this character is; that is not how *I* think!'

To think as Tolstoy's character once thought is to have my thought
processes impeded, even blocked, by a clash of oughts. On the one hand,
Caius ought to die; he is man, after all, and it is appropriate for men,
being mortal, to die. On the other hand (speaking from the character's
perspective), I ought not to die; I have thoughts, emotions; it would be
'too terrible'. There is no such clash of oughts in Heidegger's portrayal of
our everyday Being-towards-death. Again, this makes us craftier than
Tolstoy allows his character to be. In talking in terms of 'one', I can *say*,
even to myself, that my attitudes towards death are straightforward,
clear-cut, uncomplicated, upfront. This makes my facility more cunning
because it makes it more resilient, less vulnerable to demands to revise
it. Confronted by Tolstoy's reflections, for example, I can say: 'How very

confused this character is, how convoluted his self-deceptions; at least I am straight with myself!'

Tolstoy's character once thought in a combative way about death. He did not exactly evade the prospect of his own death; he 'faced' it, to the extent that he tried to argue against its possibility. But one would only have to formulate such thoughts explicitly to be immediately and embarrassingly aware of how flawed they are. Death is not something whose possibility can be argued against. Again, Heidegger portrays us as more shrewd in our everyday Being-towards-death. I can respond to Tolstoy's reflections by saying 'What obvious errors this character makes; at least I don't make the mistake of being combative towards death!' This makes it all the easier for me to maintain my attitudes unchanged, to sustain the illusion that they need no correction or revision. And this cunning puts me in a better position to conceal death's real nature from myself, to overlook or ignore the fact that it is a genuine possibility for me, non-relational, and not to be outstripped.

(ii) Ownmost

Heidegger speaks of our 'ownmost Being-towards-death'. Reversing the angle, he describes death as 'a distinctive potentiality-for-being which belongs to Dasein's ownmost self'. Thus inauthenticity in Dasein's Being-towards-death is truly drastic: 'an alienation in which its *ownmost* potentiality-for-being is hidden from it'. This is the alienation condition in its most radical form: my capacity as Dasein to hide what is most deeply myself from myself, to conceal what is most my own.

Indeed, this condition is so extreme, we may wonder about the plausibility of what Heidegger describes. Appreciating how it is possible for people ever to succeed at genuine self-deception is – notoriously – difficult enough. How can the one doing the deceiving *really* be the one being deceived, if it is *real* deception? But the difficulty of appreciating what Heidegger is proposing enters another order of magnitude altogether: that what is being hidden is not only ownmost to the one from whom it is being hidden but to the one doing the hiding, in the very event of so hiding it, and this ownmost self-hiding is commonplace.

At the very least, succeeding at this would require great cunning. Hence the importance of the contrast with the comparatively unsophisticated resources that Tolstoy ascribes to Ivan Illych. To find Heidegger's representation of our inauthenticity about death plausible, we have to assume that people really are as he imagines them to be: capable of very considerable resourcefulness, with attitudes that are very deeply resilient to counter-evidence.

(iii) Pessimism

If I really am capable of hiding from myself in this way, then that which does the hiding must reach down at least as deep as that which is hidden. And what is hidden is what is ownmost to me as Dasein, an existential and ontological rather than merely 'ontic' feature, one among the features that are most my own, something that death will reach and which is thus called on to face that death. So there is good reason to regard inauthenticity itself as among what is ownmost to me as Dasein.

We have seen evidence elsewhere that Heidegger does indeed think that inauthenticity is among what is ownmost to me as Dasein. He describes the 'falling' associated with inauthenticity as an 'ownmost inertia', 'a definite existential characteristic of Dasein itself', something that reveals Dasein's 'essential ontological structure' (184; 176; 179). His analysis of our Being-towards-death fits this deeply pessimistic picture.

What is at stake here we also know. If we combine Heidegger's account of being authentic with his deep pessimism, a number of paradoxes arise and with it the Trojan Horse predicament. We shall return to this possibility, that Heidegger is vulnerable to the same systematically self-undermining tendency as previous philosophers, once we have dealt with more minor criticisms.

3. Questions

According to Heidegger, our everyday Being-towards-death is steeped in inauthenticity. How we deal with death is revealed in and through what we tend to say about it. And what phenomenological inquiry into our preference for 'one dies' talk reveals is that Dasein tends to lose itself in the they.

As Dasein, I hide myself from the fact that my death is a genuine possibility for me, indeed my ownmost possibility, the possibility of the impossibility of any existence at all. In so doing, I also hide from myself that my death is non-relational and that my death is not to be outstripped. I do this in a variety of ways: by pretending to myself that death is an indeterminate something, that it only really strikes the they, that it is not a genuine threat to me, or by actualizing my death, setting out to expect it, to conceive it in concrete detail, or by surrendering at the prospect to passing emotions like fear.

If we are to question this analysis in a clear and helpful way, it makes sense to start with some of the more obvious and overt features before working our way down to the fundamental issues. And of the various interrelated claims that stand out in Heidegger's analysis, the most obvious and overt are three.

First, that what we tend to say 'reveals unambiguously' our everyday Being-towards-death.

Second, that what we tend to say here takes the form of 'one dies' talk.

And third, that such talk reveals the deep inauthenticity of our Being-towards-death.

(i) Should we focus on what we tend to say?

It is not news that we tend to talk around death. But we are also often silent about it. And the possibilities of this silence, the quality it may have, seem sometimes to be missing from Heidegger's analysis.

We often hold ourselves back from talking about death, or chide ourselves for having spoken, thinking 'that would have been better left unsaid'. But this is not necessarily out of fear of making ourselves uneasy or of losing our own inner comfort, let alone out of self-deception. It may be for any number of good reasons, including a creditable anxiety about being trivial or trite, a desire to be attentive rather than merely voluble, or a willingness to tend to the needs of others, respecting their anxieties, not wishing to exacerbate their concerns or to intrude on their grief, being thoughtful, avoiding insensitivity and so on.

So although we may support the first claim in the general case, we may doubt its application here. Generally speaking, what we tend to say about something may well be a good guide to our dealings with it. But there are exceptions, and one of them occurs where we knowingly and intentionally check what we say, and have good reason to do so. And death often gives us such reason.

Here perhaps, what we tend *not* to say – but naturally feel or think – may act as an equally good guide to our everyday Being-towards-death. Indeed, plausibly, it is at least equally necessary as a guide. So ignoring such evidence, as Heidegger tends to, might well skew our analysis.

(ii) What does 'one dies' talk reveal?

It may be well that, in saying things like 'I wonder what happens after one dies' and 'One dies happier in one's sleep', we are quite determinedly submerging thoughts of ourselves in the indeterminate mass of the 'the they' – whether that be the no-one-at-all, or the no-one-in-particular – so as to comfort ourselves with the illusion that death is vague, no real threat, something that belongs to anyone but somehow not to me.

But this is not necessarily the case. The occasion for these words, what draws them out of us, may equally be the deaths of people who are close to us. And where this is the occasion, our way of using 'one' may be a self-conscious way of identifying ourselves as part of a particular group whose existence as individuals is perfectly obvious and determinate to us, and whose particular deaths matter to us in all their determinate detail.

Where 'one dies' talk expresses this experience of being bound by a common concern with particular deaths, it is not at all clear that what it reveals is any sort of inauthenticity in our Being-towards-death.

(iii) What can the deaths of others reveal?

There is a larger point here, going beyond what 'one dies' talk reveals. Heidegger's analysis of our everyday Being-towards-death concentrates almost exclusively on the two extreme ends of a spectrum: our dealings with our own death, and our dealings with the deaths of those who are nothing to us but 'the they'. The rest of the spectrum seems to be largely missing. A particular blind spot is one that ought to be of considerable interest: our dealings with the deaths of those who are close to us.

Heidegger does acknowledge that the deaths of others may arouse in us a 'respectful solicitude' (238). But there are those whose deaths, even the *prospect* of whose deaths, arouse a great deal more than that. Consider the deaths of our friends and colleagues, the deaths of our loved ones, the deaths of our parents, our siblings. Our dealings with these deaths inevitably affect our everyday Being-towards-death in deep and precise ways. Heidegger rather overlooks this, and his analysis suffers as a result.

When I think about the deaths of those who are close to me – whether facing the fact that they will die some time in the future, or experiencing their dying in front of me, or dealing with the fact that they have already died – I am certainly not representing death to myself in a vague way, as *some* thing that will come from *some* where at *some* time. Where this particular person is dying – a friend, a colleague, a parent, a sibling – I think of their death as a real threat, to them and to me. Where this particular person will die, or has already died, I think of something quite specific and precise and real and determinate: the absolute loss of this living being from the world. It follows that I need not be *concealing* my ownmost death in thinking of or experiencing death as something that comes to others.

(iv) Can the deaths of others help with authenticity?

We might go further. In thinking of or experiencing the deaths of others, I may not only be drawing myself within the group of those for whom death is precise and real and determinate but I may be including myself among those to whom death belongs. By such means, I may be *exposing* myself to my own death as my non-relational, not to be outstripped, ownmost possibility.

Consider again the case where talk of the death of others represents death as belonging to the individuals that are close to me, whose particular loss is fully appreciable by me. I may come to recognize that the individuals close to me are those for whom my own death would be a similarly absolute loss as theirs would be for me. In performing this about-face, I take what I appreciate through a particularly intense way of being concerned with the deaths of others and re-deploy it to set about facing my ownmost death. In talking of death as something that comes to these others, I help awaken my sense of my ownmost death and begin exposing myself to it, in all its specific and precise and real and determinate detail.

This at least is a possibility. Not that talking of death as something that comes to others who are close to me need be sufficient of itself to awaken my sense of my ownmost death. Not that such talk is the only way of beginning to expose myself to my ownmost death. But it seems to be one way, among others, of coming to face what is particular about and peculiar to my ownmost death.

Thus, far from cultivating inauthenticity, thinking of death as something that comes to others who are close to me may defy what is tempting and tranquillizing and alienating and entangling about 'the they' talk. And far from being merely idle, or curious, or ambiguous, such thought may bear the marks of authenticity: a discourse that is properly attuned to and understanding of my own Being-towards-death, appreciating my death as my ownmost possibility, something non-relational and not to be outstripped.

(v) Heidegger and the deaths of others

If this possibility seems reasonable enough, we may wonder whether Heidegger need deny it. He may not explore how our dealings with the deaths of others may help open us to face our own ownmost death. But is this a possibility he could acknowledge?

Unfortunately, he does seem set against the idea. For example, while reminding us that death is 'a possibility-of-Being which Dasein itself has to take over in every case', Heidegger goes on:

> If Dasein stands before itself as this possibility, it has been *fully* assigned to its ownmost potentiality-for-Being. When it stands before itself in this way, all its relations to any other Dasein have been undone. This ownmost non-relational possibility is at the same time the uttermost one. (250)

Now the crucial phrase 'all its relations to any other Dasein have been undone' could be interpreted in several different ways. It may be a somewhat exaggerated way of saying what seems plausible: that facing my ownmost death is radically different from dealing with death as it comes to others. But many assume, with textual justification, that Heidegger has something much more extreme in mind: that facing my ownmost death requires cutting myself off from all vestiges of my dealings with death as it comes to others, that there is nothing about the latter which might enable it to act as a point of transition, a way of coming to the former.

If so, two distinct issues arise. One we have already explored a little here. Given that we may plausibly learn much about our ownmost death from thinking about and experiencing the deaths of those close to us, it is difficult to see what could possibly motivate such a drastic form of isolationism.

The other issue also relies on what we now know, but much more broadly, since it takes into account the full story as it has been laid out in the previous two chapters. It is difficult to see how such isolationism could be made consistent with Heidegger's whole orientation in *Being and Time*.

Part of the point of insisting that I conceive myself as Da-Sein, always already being-there, is to refuse all temptation to lapse back into conceiving of myself as an isolated, free-floating unit. And Heidegger is nowhere more emphatic about this than in the analysis of authenticity. For him, being authentic necessarily brings Dasein into a current, concernful and solicitous Being-with others (298). Hence it seems oddly inconsistent of Heidegger to deny that Being-with plays a similarly essential role when, as Dasein, I am authentic in my Being-towards-death.

4. Trojan Horse syndrome

So we may question the evidence on which Heidegger constructs his analysis of everyday Being-towards-death. It may well be that he systematically ignores perfectly viable ways of coming to face our ownmost death, for example through facing the deaths of those close to us. Perhaps he allows his conclusion to determine what he counts as evidence for it. It may also be that, were Heidegger to acknowledge the crucial role that concernful and solicitous Being-with others may play in enabling us to face our ownmost death, he would adopt an analysis that accords more satisfactorily not only with our lived experience but also with his own overall orientation.

Be that as it may, a deeper problem looms. Heidegger may be drawing into the heart of his position a set of commitments that undermines his own most fundamental efforts, thus falling for the Trojan Horse.

(i) The predicament

We are already aware of the essence of the predicament. It comes about because of two core elements of Heidegger's position: his account of being authentic and his deep pessimism. If we agree that being authentic is a matter of being what is 'ownmost' to me, while also accepting that being inauthentic is among what is 'ownmost' to me, various contradictions seem to result: that it is authentic for me to be inauthentic and inauthentic for me to be authentic, and that failing to be what is ownmost to me is itself what is ownmost to me.

To be more meticulous about this, it seems that Heidegger's commitments here generate at least two specific paradoxes. One is a paradox of being: that, being Dasein, I am both inauthentic and authentic, at the same time and in the deepest sense. The other is a paradox of philosophy: that, being Dasein, I both am and cannot be an appropriate point of access for philosophy.

If Heidegger's commitments do indeed generate these paradoxes, then it seems he falls for the Trojan Horse, like other philosophers (Descartes, Locke, Marx, Adorno) before him. This predicament is the more poignant because it is precisely to avoid this systematically self-undermining tendency of previous philosophizing that Heidegger adopts such strenuous means to re-enter philosophy.

Finally, we know this predicament is general as well as deep. It threatens Heidegger's position on how we face life just as much as it threatens his position on how we face death. Hopefully, we have now gathered sufficient resources to address this issue full on. This is not just a matter of knowing enough to identify where the pressure points lie, but of being sensitive enough to appreciate where Heidegger must be firm and where he can be flexible.

(ii) The ontic option

When we first encountered the predicament, a remedy may have suggested itself. If only Heidegger could renounce his deep pessimism and treat inauthenticity as a more superficial feature of Dasein, something less than 'ownmost' to me. Might he not then escape the paradoxes?

We should first be clear about this option and what it involves. Using Heidegger's own terminology, it turns on the difference between treating inauthenticity as an 'ontological' feature and as an 'ontic' feature.

Consider the claim that, as Dasein, I am constantly liable to being inauthentic. If we interpret this as an *ontological* claim, it would mean inauthenticity is a fundamental existential feature of the Being I am. Without my inauthenticity, I would not be the Being I am. Inauthenticity would rank alongside other fundamental existential features of mine as Dasein: that this Being is mine, that I am related understandingly in my Being towards my own Being, that I am situated, that my Being is grounded in the unitary phenomenon Being-in-the-world.

But we might interpret the claim very differently, as an *ontic* claim. After all, to say that I am constantly liable to being inauthentic, as Dasein, leaves room for the *possibility* of my being the Being that I am and yet *not* inauthentic. Nothing fundamental or existential about me need change if that were so. To say this is to claim that inauthenticity is a contingent feature of the Being that I am, something that may but need not be the case for me. Note: it is not to claim that it is probable or even likely that I am or ever will be authentic. It does not change the fact – if it is a fact – that being inauthentic is deeply ingrained in me. Someone convinced of Heidegger's analysis would insist on this. They might even claim that being inauthentic is all-but-unavoidable for me, as Dasein. Still, the point is that I might still be the Being I am without being inauthentic. I would survive the change if that change consisted in my no longer being inauthentic.

We can spell out this ontic option for the specific case of my Being-towards-death. Being Dasein, I am always already situated in relation to my ownmost death. But I am also constantly liable to being inauthentic about this. In particular, I am vulnerable to a variety of ways of denying, ignoring or evading my ownmost death. Hence I tend to be false to my own Being, as Dasein. But since this tendency is a contingent feature of mine, something that may but need not be the case and hence is neither fundamental nor existential to me, I might still be the Being I am without being inauthentic in my Being-towards-death. The ontic option leaves room for this possibility.

(iii) The ontic option and the paradoxes

Whether it would be consistent for Heidegger to adopt the ontic option is an issue to which we shall return. We should first ascertain whether it would be worth his doing so. And the primary consideration is this: whether the ontic option would generate the paradoxes that put Heidegger in his predicament, or whether it enables him to resolve these paradoxes and thus escape the Trojan Horse.

The prospect is certainly hopeful. Heidegger could retain his position on authenticity: that being authentic is essentially a matter of being what is ownmost to me, what belongs to me as most proper to me, most peculiar to me. But he could modify his position on inauthenticity. If being inauthentic is a contingent feature of the Being that I am, it would no longer be among what is ownmost to me. Hence the contradictory positions would no longer arise. It would no longer be inauthentic for me to be authentic. And failing to be what is ownmost to me would no longer be what is ownmost to me.

Proceeding more meticulously, we can see just how it is that the ontic option enables Heidegger to escape the paradoxes to which the alternative 'ontological' option would surrender him.

The paradox of being arises because Heidegger holds both (1) being authentic is essentially a matter of being what is ownmost to me, and (2) being inauthentic is among what is ownmost to me, as Dasein. But embracing the ontic interpretation, he can deny (2). Thus he can accept what seems obvious, that (3) it cannot be that I am being both authentic and inauthentic at the same time and in the same deepest sense. Moreover, he can imagine that (4) I am being authentic in the deepest sense at time T. And he can accept what follows from (1), (3) and (4), that (5) I cannot be being inauthentic in the deepest sense at T. Indeed, he can accept what follows from (1) and (4), that (6) I am being what is ownmost to me at T. The point is that, having denied (2), Heidegger can deny that (7) I am being inauthentic in the deepest sense at T. In short, he avoids the paradox of being because he is no longer committed to *both* (5) and (7).

The paradox of philosophy also depends on a claim that Heidegger can reject, if he embraces the ontic interpretation. He can continue to endorse his audacious optimism, which arises out of his commitment to the claims that (1) The proper task of philosophy is to raise the question of the meaning of Being, (2) we require the phenomenological method to perform this task, which is 'to let that which shows itself be seen from itself in the very way in which it shows itself from itself', and (3) as Dasein, I am such that Being is always and already in question for me. Heidegger takes (1)–(3) to show that (4) as Dasein, I am an appropriate point of access for philosophy, turned towards whatever shows itself in me, able to see it in the very way it shows itself in me. The point is that, having embraced the ontic interpretation, Heidegger can deny that (5) being inauthentic is among what is ownmost to me, as Dasein. So he can continue to hold that (6) to be inauthentic is for me to fail to bring myself 'face to face' with myself, to 'turn away' from myself in accordance with my 'ownmost inertia of falling', without concluding that (7) as Dasein, I *cannot* be an appropriate point of access for philosophy. In short, Heidegger avoids the paradox of philosophy because he is no longer committed to *both* (4) and (7). Being inauthentic is a contingent feature of mine, no matter how ingrained. It is possible for me to be the Being I am and not inauthentic. Hence nothing here contradicts (4), that I am, as Dasein, an appropriate point of access for philosophy. Being the Being I am, it is possible that Being is always and already a question for me (3) in such a way that I am turned towards whatever shows itself in me, able to see it in the very way it shows itself in me, and hence I am the appropriate point of access for the phenomenological method (2), the method which is necessary to perform the proper task of philosophy (1).

Notice that, in taking the ontic option, Heidegger not only avoids the paradoxes of being and philosophy but also protects his optimistic re-entry into philosophy. As Dasein, I *can* be the appropriate point of access for the phenomenological method. And if philosophy can use this point of access to raise the question of the meaning of Being, it can escape the characteristic failures of previous philosophizing. Thus the ontic option enables Heidegger to accomplish two related tasks: revealing what is systematically self-defeating about previous philosophy while avoiding the Trojan Horse himself.

(iv) The ontic option and audacity

There is an additional positive aspect to the optic option. It opens up the possibility of a strikingly optimistic audacity in practical matters that would match Heidegger's optimistic audacity in theoretical matters.

We have just reminded ourselves of the theoretical form of this optimistic audacity: the claim that, as Dasein, I am myself an appropriate point of access for philosophy. This is optimistic and audacious because it means that we need only exploit the situation we are already in to achieve what we seek. The same may be said of the corresponding practical form of optimistic audacity, which the ontic interpretation would make available.

We can begin by admitting that, as Dasein, I am constantly liable to being inauthentic. In particular, I am constantly liable to deny, ignore or evade my own death. This is one relevant element, which we interpret ontically. The second element we interpret ontologically, because it represents a fundamental existential feature of mine: that, as Dasein, I am a being whose being it is to inquire into Being. Putting these two elements together, one ontic and one ontological, we are free to acknowledge a certain possibility: that pursuing this inquiry into Being, I may come to understand and perhaps even resolve my tendency to evade my own death. In pursuing what is ontological about myself, I may come to understand and even resolve something ontic about myself. And if this is a possibility, then I may be, as Dasein, both the problem and the means to resolve it. Once again, therefore, we may achieve what we seek in exploiting the very situation we are already. That is the cause for optimism and audacity in the ontic interpretation.

(v) The ontic and ontological options

So there is much to recommend the ontic option. To ascribe my inauthenticity to a tendency of mine that is not ontological would enable

Heidegger to continue separating himself firmly from the commitments that undermine previous philosophizing, thus protecting himself from the Trojan Horse. And it would enable him to match his audacious optimism in theoretical matters with the same stance towards practical matters.

We may be confident, having reviewed the textual evidence in the previous chapter, that Heidegger himself does not adopt the ontic option. Speaking of the 'falling' that denotes inauthenticity, he says categorically that it 'reveals an essential ontological structure of Dasein itself' (179), that it 'constitutes all Dasein's days in their everydayness' (179) and that this 'inertia' is an ownmost feature of Dasein (184). The evidence points unequivocally towards the ontological option.

But that does not settle the issue entirely. It is necessary to ask whether it would be *open* to Heidegger to adopt the ontic option. Not if he were to stick by the claims recalled in the previous paragraph, granted. Still, an obliging thought may arise: that these claims represent a negotiable part of his overall position, something that he could reasonably renounce, if forced, without significant loss or change to his core position. And we ought to entertain this obliging thought, given how much there is to recommend the ontic option, and – what presses more urgently – how disastrous it would be to maintain the alternative. Indeed, it may seem obvious that anyone pursuing Heidegger's overall design has no real choice: they must take the ontic option. It would mean deeply revising the account of inauthenticity, but better that alternative, so one will think, than renouncing the core position.

Unfortunately, the ontic option really is not open to Heidegger. Adopting it would mean not just revising his account of inauthenticity but also rejecting the core of his position: his analysis of our everyday Being-towards-death. For consider the two essential claims on which this analysis rests: that, as Dasein, I tend to 'cover over' and 'hide' my Being-towards-death and that my Being-towards-death is among that which is ownmost to me (e.g. 253). If the first claim is true, my inauthenticity must be at least as fundamental a feature of mine as my Being-towards-death. Otherwise it could not succeed in 'covering over' or 'hiding' my Being-towards-death. And if the second claim is true, my Being-towards-death must be an ontological feature of mine. This follows from Heidegger's own definitions of what is ownmost and what is ontological. So, as Dasein, my inauthenticity must be an ontological feature of mine. Heidegger has every reason to insist on this, it turns out, just as we have seen him do.

Heidegger is in a bind, so it appears. He can only escape the Trojan Horse by taking the ontic option. But this means rejecting his analysis of our everyday Being-towards-death. And this is not an alternative to renouncing his core position. It just is to renounce it.

5. Possible paths to pursue

Sections 50–3 of *Being and Time* contain the heart of Heidegger's 'preliminary' existential analysis of our Being-towards-death. Sections 46–9 set this analysis in context. With time to the fore, Heidegger is able to identify the 'ontological meaning' of care with temporality, which considerably complicates his earlier identification of Dasein's Being with care. It is helpful to pursue the discussion of authenticity through this change of approach by reading on through sections 54–60 on resoluteness and conscience and through sections 61–6 on temporality and the ontological meaning of care.

The Kierkegaard of *Concluding Unscientific Postscript* was a peculiarly deep influence on Heidegger in his dealings with both death and authenticity, though the minimal references to him rather disguise the fact. The 'excursus' on Kierkegaard in Stephen Mulhall's *Heidegger and Being and Time* (chapter 5) is an insightful reflection on these connections. Taylor Carman's account of Heidegger on death and (in)authenticity has undergone revision since his *Heidegger's Analytic* (chapter 6), but this remains a helpful initial discussion. Edith Stein was the first to identify Heidegger's blind spot about the death of others who are close to us, a most important element in her critical essay 'Martin Heideggers Existenzphilosophie' (published as yet only in German, as an appendix to her main work *Endliches und Ewiges Sein*). Stein was peculiarly well placed to spot this flaw, not just because she was also a student and later assistant of Husserl and knew Heidegger, but because empathy had been the focus of her earlier work in phenomenology. For helpful reflection on the interconnections, see Alasdair Macintyre's *Edith Stein: A Philosophical Prologue* (chapter 17) and Judith Wolfe's *Heidegger and Theology* (chapter 8).

Next steps

The underlying aim of this book has been simple and practical: to enable us to address the momentous crises of present days by facing up to the fundamental questions that previous radical philosophers have raised, to think along with them, drawing what is valuable from their example and letting go of what is false, with the aim of puzzling through to some answers of our own.

So I shall soon be getting out of the way.

What follows are some final, open-ended reflections, intended to cast a more positive light on the place in which we now find ourselves.

1. Where we are

We need philosophy to be radical if it is to stay relevant and connected. But this urge to be radical threatens to undermine philosophy itself.

We have met time and again with this paradox. When philosophers become audacious, get to the roots of things and are thoroughly engaged with fundamental issues that matter to us all, they tend to drag commitments into the heart of their position that destroy it.

We have not just observed this tendency in exploring five very different ways of being radical in philosophy. We have experienced it from within. For our approach throughout has been to philosophize ourselves, to face the fundamental issues that philosophers face, to work alongside them.

To recognize this self-undermining tendency may seem sad and depressing. But this need not be so. Looked at another way, it is both liberating and invigorating. When we experience the difficulties other philosophers face, this can stimulate us to begin developing our own philosophical analyses of life and death.

Consider the particular problem at which we have just arrived, for example. If we are audacious enough, we may find a radical route out of it.

2. Paradox

The problem is this. Either we reject Heidegger's analysis of our everyday Being-towards-death or we reject his analysis of our inauthenticity. Either way, we need to make a new start at getting to the roots of things.

But we may be overlooking a feature of the overall situation. If we can extricate ourselves from the immediate details and gain a little distance, this feature reveals itself more clearly. What threatens Heidegger is paradox, most sharply in his attempts to analyse our Being-towards-death. And we have been assuming what in normal circumstances is valid: that an analysis that generates paradoxes must be rejected as unsound. But perhaps these are not normal circumstances.

There is something special about death, after all. Many philosophers have sought to capture this by saying that death itself just is paradoxical. This is a quintessentially radical claim, of course: it is audacious about fundamental issues that matter to us all. And explaining why and how this claim might be true is notoriously difficult. But what matters for the moment is simply what might follow: that the statements we formulate when thinking about death will naturally and unavoidably contradict each other. This will not be a sign of weakness in our insights or failure in our reasoning. Indeed, if death just is paradoxical, the more deeply and rigorously we try to philosophize about it, the more these contradictions will accrue.

So we will not reject Heidegger's analysis of our Being-towards-death simply on the grounds that it generates paradoxes. We would expect a sound analysis of this particular subject to do just that. Indeed, it is the analyses that fail to generate paradoxes that we would reject as unsound. Given that death just is paradoxical, to formulate statements about it that do not contradict each other would reveal that one's insights must be weak or one's reasoning faulty.

Of course, this move will only help *Heidegger* if his analysis is open to treating death itself as paradoxical. We may think he is proposing precisely this when he insists – frequently – that where death is concerned,

> what the understanding needs to penetrate is the possibility of the impossibility of any existence at all. (262; all page references in this conclusion are to Martin Heidegger's *Being and Time*; see the Bibliography for full details)

This has the air of paradox about it, at least if we assume it is asking us to understand that the same thing at the same time is both possible and impossible. But Heidegger may well have something less straightforwardly contradictory in mind. In the general case, after all, we are quite capable of understanding the possibility that such-and-such is impossible. I am not contradicting myself when I say 'It is possible that the existence of a wholly authentic human being is impossible', for instance.

Still, Heidegger does use cautionary phrasing here: 'what the understanding needs to penetrate'. If this indicates a difficulty for our minds to overcome, what is it?

The struggle here has partly to do with the sheer difficulty of genuinely treating a possibility *as* a possibility. Heidegger thinks we tend to treat what is possible as if it were actually already available to us. Unless we overcome this powerful tendency by adopting an attitude of 'expectancy', keeping possibility as precisely what is *not* (yet) available, we do not just distort but 'annihilate' the character of possibility altogether (261).

All well and good. But this is a general point that presumably applies to genuinely treating *any* possibility as a possibility. What adds to the element of struggle here is partly the fact that death faces me with a particular, enhanced possibility: what Heidegger calls my 'uttermost possibility' (259). And another cause of difficulty is the nature of that which is to be treated as my uttermost possibility: 'the absolute impossibility of existence' (255).

Why does Heidegger insist on the enhanced terms here: 'uttermost' and 'absolute'? Evidently, he is reaching for more than the commonplace thoughts that abound in this area – that it is difficult for me to imagine the world without me in it, for example. Or rather, such familiar puzzles take on a peculiarly acute form for Heidegger, given his joint analyses of Dasein and our Being-towards-death.

3. Minimalism

We can frame the issue here in terms of the tension between three claims.

First, my death is my ownmost, non-relational and not to be outstripped *Not-Being-There*.

Second, I am always already situated in relation to my own death.

Third, I am always already Da-Sein, *Being-There*, grounded in the unitary phenomenon Being-in-the-world.

The peculiarly strong conception of death in the first claim helps explain Heidegger's enhanced depiction of it as 'the absolute impossibility of existence'. And what helps explain his enhanced depiction of my death as my 'uttermost possibility' is the fact that he regards the second and third claims as among what is ownmost to me, as Dasein.

The struggle – 'what the understanding needs to penetrate' – is how to hold all three claims together. If I am always already *Being-There* and my death is my *Not-Being-There*, surely I could never be situated in relation to my death? Indeed, any two of the claims go well together, but they always point to the negation of the third. Perhaps I am always already situated in relation to my death, and my death is my *Not-Being-There*. But then, surely, I could not be always already *Being-There*? Perhaps I am always already *Being-There*, always already situated in relation to my death. But then, surely, death could not be my *Not-Being-There*?

Notice that the struggle here has nothing directly to do with authenticity or inauthenticity. Even if we radically change Heidegger's views about our Being-towards-death so as to adopt the ontic option, the contradictions would remain.

But perhaps it is not so very clear that they *are* contradictions.

Consider the first way of posing the issue: if I am always already *Being-There* and my death is my *Not-Being-There*, I could never be situated in relation to my death. Now what makes it plausible to assume this is that we conceive my death in a particular way. There is 'something' my death is; an indeterminate something, no doubt, but 'there' in a way that makes sense for me to think of it as forever beyond me, beyond what I am capable of situating myself in relation to.

But we might reject this way of conceiving my death. Heidegger himself gives us reason. Part of his aim is to root out the idea that my death is

> an indefinite something which, above all, must duly arrive from somewhere or other, but which is proximally *not yet objectively present* for oneself. (253)

Such a conception essentially disarms death, Heidegger notes, denying what is essential: its capacity to be a *threat* for me.

Recognizing this prompts us to ask whether there is a conception of death under which Heidegger's three claims might turn out to be true together. Perhaps there is.

Suppose, for example, that there is *nothing* my death is, no 'something' for it to be and no 'there' where it remains beyond me. *All* there is to my death is my ownmost, non-relational and not to be outstripped *Not-Being-There*. And suppose my grasping this just *is* for me to be situated in relation to my own death. To grasp this about my death is to grasp all there is to grasp. Then perhaps my understanding penetrates what it needs to penetrate: a way of *Being-There* that is always already situated in relation to my *Not-Being-There*. As regards my death, to be situated in relation to this is to be situated in relation to all there is to be situated in relation to. Within this minimalism about death, all three claims turn out to be true together. And this minimalism is again quintessentially radical.

So we have choices, routes we may pursue out of the current impasse:

We might propose that death itself just is paradoxical.

We might propose minimalism about death.

We might propose a more thoroughgoing revision of the underlying analysis.

To think carefully about such proposals and to consider endorsing them is not to shy away from philosophy's urge to be radical, to engage with the concrete, fundamental problems of living, working, thinking and dying. Quite the opposite. It is to be audacious and engaged with fundamental issues that matter to us all about how the world is and how we should live in it.

To the radical philosophizing then.

Bibliography

Main Texts

Adorno, Theodor (2005) *Minima Moralia*, tr. E. F. N. Jephcott (London: Verso).

Descartes, René (1984) *Meditations on First Philosophy, The Philosophical Writings of Descartes*, tr. John Cottingham, Robert Stoothoff and Dugald Murdoch, Volume II (Cambridge: Cambridge University Press).

Descartes, René (1985) *Discourse on the Method, The Philosophical Writings of Descartes*, tr. John Cottingham, Robert Stoothoff and Dugald Murdoch, Volume I (Cambridge: Cambridge University Press).

Heidegger, Martin (1962) *Being and Time*, 7th edition, tr. John Macquarrie and Edward Robinson (Oxford: Blackwell). In-text page numbers refer to the German edition as is standard, for ease of reference across the original and other translations. These numbers are given at the sides of the page in the Macquarrie-Robinson and Stambaugh translations.

Locke, John (1975) *An Essay Concerning Human Understanding*, ed. P. Nidditch (Oxford: Oxford University Press).

Marx, Karl (1971) *Economic and Philosophical Manuscripts of 1844* (Paris Manuscripts) in *Karl Marx: Early Texts*, tr. David McLellan (Oxford: Blackwell), 130–83.

Further Reading

Adorno, Theodor (1964) *The Jargon of Authenticity*, tr. Knut Tarnowski and Frederic Will (Evanstown: Northwestern University Press, 1973).

Adorno, Theodor and Horkheimer, Max (1947) *Dialectic of Enlightenment*, tr. John Cumming (London: Verso, 1979).

Agamben, Giorgio (2002) *The Open: Man and Animal*, tr. Kevin Attell (Stanford: Stanford University Press, 2004).

Alanen, Lilli (2003) *Descartes' Concept of Mind* (Cambridge, MA: Harvard University Press).

Ayers, Michael (1991) *Locke: Epistemology and Ontology* (London: Routledge).

Bernhard, Thomas (1985) *Old Masters: A Comedy*, tr. Ewald Osers (Chicago: The University of Chicago Press).

Blattner, William (2013) 'Authenticity and Resoluteness', in M. Wrathall (ed.), *The Cambridge Companion to Being and Time* (Cambridge: Cambridge University Press).

Broughton, Janet (2002) *Descartes' Method of Doubt* (Princeton: Princeton University Press).

Buck-Morss, Susan (1977) *The Origin of Negative Dialectics: Theodor W. Adorno, Walter Benjamin and the Frankfurt Institute* (Sussex: The Harvester Press).

Burnyeat, Myles and Frede, Michael, eds (1998) *The Original Sceptics: A Controversy* (Indianapolis: Hackett).

Carman, Taylor (2003) *Heidegger' Analytic* (Cambridge: Cambridge University Press).

Cassam, Quassim (2022) *Extremism: A Philosophical Analysis* (London: Routledge).

Chappell, Vere, ed. (1998) *Locke* (Oxford: Oxford University Press).

Cohen, G. A. (1978) *Karl Marx's Theory of History: A Defence*, expanded version (Oxford: Oxford University Press, 2000).

Cottingham, John (1986) *Descartes* (Oxford: Blackwell).

Craig, Edward (1987) *The Mind of God and the Works of Man* (Oxford: Oxford University Press).

Dancy, Jonathan (1985) *Introduction to Contemporary Epistemology* (Oxford: Blackwell).

Derrida, Jacques (1987) *Of Spirit*, tr. Geoffrey Bennington and Rachel Bowlby (Chicago: University of Chicago Press, 1989).

Elster, Jon (1985) *Making Sense of Marx* (Cambridge: Cambridge University Press).

Elster, Jon (1986) *An Introduction to Karl Marx* (Cambridge: Cambridge University Press).

Friedman, Michael (2000) *A Parting of the Ways: Carnap, Cassirer and Heidegger* (Chicago: Open Court).

Foster, John (1991) *The Immaterial Self* (London: Routledge).

Gaukroger, Stephen (1995) *Descartes: An Intellectual Biography* (Oxford: Oxford University Press).

Gordon, Peter (2010) *Continental Divide: Heidegger, Cassirer, Davos* (Cambridge, MA: Harvard University Press).

Gordon, Peter (2016) *Adorno and Existence* (Cambridge, MA: Harvard University Press).

Heidegger, Martin (1923) *Ontology—The Hermeneutics of Facticity*, tr. John van Buren (Bloomington: Indiana University Press, 1999).

Heidegger, Martin (1924) *Introduction to Phenomenological Research*, tr. Daniel Dahlstrom (Bloomington: Indiana University Press, 2005).

Heidegger, Martin (1930) *The Fundamental Concepts of Metaphysics*, tr. William McNeill and Nicholas Walker (Bloomington: Indiana University Press, 1995).

Heil, John (1986) *Philosophy of Mind* (London: Routledge).

Jaeggi, Rahel (2015) *Alienation*, tr. Frederick Neuhouser and Alan E. Smith (New York: Columbia University Press).

Jay, Martin (1973) *The Dialectical Imagination: A History of the Frankfurt School and the Institute of Social Research* (London: University of California Press).

Kenny, Anthony (1968) *Descartes: A Study of his Philosophy Reprinted* (New York: Random House).

Kenny, Anthony (1989) *The Metaphysics of Mind* (Oxford: Oxford University Press).

Kierkegaard, Søren (1846) *Concluding Unscientific Postscript*, tr. H. V. Hong and E. H. Hong (Princeton: Princeton University Press, 1992).

Liedman, Sven-Eric (2018) *A World to Win: The Life and Works of Karl Marx*, tr. Jeffrey N. Skinner (London: Verso).

Lowe, E. J. (1995) *Locke on Human Understanding* (London: Routledge).

Macintyre, Alasdair (2006) *Edith Stein: A Philosophical Prologue* (London: Continuum).

Marx, Karl (1845) *The Holy Family* (Oxford: Blackwell).

Marx, Karl (1867) *Capital*, Volume I, tr. Ben Fowkes, ed. Ernest Mandel (London: Penguin, 1976).

McLellan, David, ed. (1977) *Karl Marx: Selected Writings* (Oxford: Oxford University Press).

McLellan, David (1977) *Karl Marx: His Life and Thought* (London: Flamingo).

Moore, Adrian (2011) *The Evolution of Modern Metaphysics: Making Sense of Things* (Cambridge: Cambridge University Press).

Mulhall, Stephen (1996) *Heidegger and Being and Time*, 2nd edition (London: Routledge, 2005).

Mulhall, Stephen (2005) *Philosophical Myths of the Fall* (Princeton: Princeton University Press).

Müller-Doohm, Stefan (2003) *Adorno: A Biography*, tr. Rodney Livingstone (London: Polity Press, 2005).

O'Connor, Brian (2012) *Adorno* (London: Routledge).

Ott, Hugo (1988) *Martin Heidegger: A Political Life*, tr. Allan Blunden (London: Fontana Press, 1993).

Plamenatz, John (1963) *Man and Society III: Hegel, Marx and Engels, and the Idea of Progress*, revised edition (London: Longman, 1992).

Popkin, Richard (1979) *History of Scepticism: From Erasmus to Spinoza* (Berkeley: University of California Press).

Robinson, Howard (2003) 'Dualism', in S. Stich and T. Warfield (eds), *The Blackwell Guide to Philosophy of Mind* (Oxford: Blackwell).

Rose, Gillian (1978) *The Melancholy Science: An Introduction to the Thought of Theodor W. Adorno* (London: Macmillan).

Rosen, Michael (1996) *Of Voluntary Servitude* (Cambridge: Polity Press).

Rozemond, Marleen (1998) *Descartes' Dualism* (Cambridge, MA: Harvard University Press).

Ryle, Gilbert (1949) *The Concept of Mind* (London: Penguin).

Safranski, Rüdiger (1994) *Martin Heidegger: Between Good and Evil*, tr. Ewald Osers (Cambridge, MA: Harvard University Press, 1998).

Singer, Peter (1983) *Hegel* (Oxford: Oxford University Press).

Stein, Edith (2006) *Endliches und Ewiges Sein* (Freiburg: Herder).

Strawson, P. F. (1959) *Individuals: An Essay in Descriptive Metaphysics* (London: Methuen and Co. Ltd).

Tolstoy, Leo (1906) 'The Death of Ivan Illych', in *The Raid and Other Stories*, tr. Louise and Aylmer Maude (Oxford: Oxford University Press).

Wheen, Francis (1999) *Karl Marx* (London: Fourth Estate).

Wiggershaus, Rolf (1986) *The Frankfurt School*, tr. Michael Robertson (Cambridge, MA: MIT Press, 1994).

Williams, Bernard (1978) *Descartes: The Project of Pure Inquiry* (London: Penguin).

Wilson, Margaret (1978) *Descartes* (London: Routledge and Kegan Paul).

Wolfe, Judith (2014) *Heidegger and Theology* (London: Bloomsbury).

Index